My MSAdventures

(pronounced "mis-adventures")

Multiple Sclerosis:
It's Not Just a Disease—It's an Adventure!

My MSAdventures
(pronounced "mis-adventures")

BECKY KENNEDY

BALBOA.
PRESS
A DIVISION OF HAY HOUSE

Balboa Press books may be ordered through booksellers or by contacting:

Balboa Press
A Division of Hay House
1663 Liberty Drive
Bloomington, IN 47403
www.balboapress.com
1-(877) 407-4847

Because of the dynamic nature of the Internet, any web addresses or links contained in this book may have changed since publication and may no longer be valid. The views expressed in this work are solely those of the author and do not necessarily reflect the views of the publisher, and the publisher hereby disclaims any responsibility for them.

The author of this book does not dispense medical advice or prescribe the use of any technique as a form of treatment for physical, emotional, or medical problems without the advice of a physician, either directly or indirectly. The intent of the author is only to offer information of a general nature to help you in your quest for emotional and spiritual well-being. In the event you use any of the information in this book for yourself, which is your constitutional right, the author and the publisher assume no responsibility for your actions.

Any people depicted in stock imagery provided by Thinkstock are models, and such images are being used for illustrative purposes only. Certain stock imagery © Thinkstock.

Printed in the United States of America

ISBN: 978-1-4525-6641-2 (sc)
ISBN: 978-1-4525-6642-9 (e)
ISBN: 978-1-4525-6643-6 (hc)

Library of Congress Control Number: 2013900091

Balboa Press rev. date: 1/14/2013

Dedication

This book is lovingly dedicated to my:

Darling daughter, Laura, for all the joy you've brought into my life.

Loving husband, Steve, for all the ramps you've built to lift me up.

Sister, Jane, for always being there for me.

Brother, Dave, my webmaster and constant support through my life.

Friends:

> LuAnn, for showing me how to laugh at my struggles.
>
> Judy, your patience and support helped me through every page.
>
> Kay, for always listening and caring.
>
> Lorette, for showing me how to be a strong, independent woman even in a wheelchair.

All the other angels in my life who have stayed by my side through this adventure.

Foreword

The diagnosis of multiple sclerosis frequently carries along fears and misconceptions, and patients who receive that diagnosis are often insufficiently counseled on what to expect. Internet has now become a great source of information and typically all sorts of answers including those that do not apply to single individuals could be found there.

The author of this book, on the other hand, has been living the troubles that come with the disease and she shares her experiences and her views with an emphasis on how to move forward. In fact, Becky, a person with a reserved and shy personality could have easily sat back and given up on living an active life, and instead, notwithstanding the physical limitations, she carries on and here she describes in humorous tones, the struggles she has to face to accomplish otherwise simple tasks.

The initiative to write this book stems from Becky's ability to look at herself and, despite the rapid accumulation of disability, to turn on the right, positive attitude.

This strength of hers becomes her motivator and here is a message of encouragement that she wants to communicate to patients not only with multiple sclerosis but also with other neurological diseases.

However, beyond being part of the literature meant for neurological patients, teaching them how to feel alive, there is an amazing load of humanity that transpires through the lines. These humanistic aspects will break boundaries and will render it a companion book enjoyable for everyone.

Roberto Bomprezzi, Neurologist, MD, PhD
MaineGeneral Neurology

Table of Contents

About the Author

Becky is a vibrant woman with dreams and courage who has been diagnosed with MS (multiple sclerosis). She lives with Steve, her husband of thirty years, in Phoenix, AZ. Previously they lived in Houston, TX, where they worked at the Johnson Space Center supporting the Space Shuttle Program with Astronaut Training and in Mission Control. While in Houston they enjoyed racing a small sailboat. Becky also served in the Coast Guard Reserves performing search and rescue activities.

After moving to Phoenix, while pursuing a successful career in the computer industry, Becky developed MS. Since this is a progressively disabling disease, her active lifestyle became increasingly challenged. Every task became an adventure, or Mis-Adventure as some turned out.

The increasing disability became more and more disheartening; the mis-adventures depressing. After her friend helped her laugh through a situation, Becky found a new way of dealing with her life's disadvantages. From then on she determined to put humor back into her life. This helped to lift the dark cloud of depression.

Despite having MS, Becky remains active in the Women's Programs at their church. She and Steve enjoy eating pizza while watching Science Fiction movies and following the NASCAR races on TV. Their daughter, Laura, is a television newscaster in Billings, Montana. She is quite the adventurous young woman herself.

After a serious bout with pneumonia and subsequent stays in rehab hospitals, Becky currently lives in a small Group Care Home. There she pushes herself through physical therapy and daily exercises with weights to improve her strength. Her goal is to return home soon.

Becky has shared her story with many friends and groups. She hopes to reach others diagnosed with MS or families supporting them through this book. It is meant to encourage those who have similar disadvantages, offer family and friends more understanding, and at least provide a laugh or two. Follow along with her on her MSAdventures as she tries to keep a positive attitude and her sense of humor through it all.

http://mymsadventures.net
becky@mymsadventures.net

Introduction

In 1993 I was diagnosed with MS, Multiple Sclerosis. As the disease progressed, it became more and more difficult to stay positive and keep my sense of humor. When I wrote to a good friend in an email about my experience one day, she replied with a humorous interpretation of it. She helped me see a different way of looking at it.

From then on as things happened, I tried to think of how I could tell her about it to make her laugh. I found that I was not as worried and stressed if I thought that way. I decided to look at MS differently, as more of an adventure – or misadventure, as it sometimes turned out.

The process of writing about my MSAdventures (pronounced "mis-adventures") this way helped me stay more positive about my life. This book is a collection of these MSAdventures over about a five year period, not necessarily in chronological order. I hope they give you a little insight into what it's like to live with this disease and how you might look at life a little differently.

The actual progression of my disease is outlined in "My MS Timeline" on the following page.

My MS Timeline

1993   Initial MS diagnosis, age 42, optic neuritis, right eye

1999   Left knee limp
Started subcutaneous shot (under skin); daily
Used for relapsing/remitting MS

2000   Second opinion; recommended drug change
Began using cane

2001   Switched to inter-muscular shot (into thigh); Once/wk. Used for secondary progressive MS

2003   Right leg became increasingly weak

2004   Stopped driving

2005   Switched to new inter-muscular shot (into thigh); 3 x/wk
New neurologist

2006   Changed from cane to walker

2007   Fell, injured head; Changed to wheelchair

2009   New neurologist, IV drug 3/09, Rehab; IV drug 4/09, Rehab, pneumonia

2010   IV drug 12/10

2012   Hospitalized with pneumonia; rehab; group
        home
        New neurologist

This was my disease progression. MS affects each person
differently.

My MSAdventures

◄◄ ◇◇◇ ►►

The Adventures Begin

How Did I Get Here?

There I was, sitting at my computer at work one afternoon. As a database administrator, my team was responsible for storing, accessing and backing up the data for a large corporation.

As I worked, my computer screen seemed to be dirty; I was having trouble seeing it clearly. I finally realized that the problem wasn't with my computer screen - it was with my eyes!

Looking out of my right eye, it looked like a window shade was closing from the top of my eye. The bottom of the shade was just below the center of my vision. I could see clearly below the edge of the "shade", but directly in front or above was a grey blur.

I started to panic, and then called my ophthalmologist. It was almost 4pm. I knew the office would be closing soon, but they agreed to see me if I came right away. The office was only a couple of miles away, but rush-hour traffic was already clogging the streets. So here I was, hurrying through traffic with a vision problem – not the safest thing to do. I couldn't imagine what horrible things were happening inside my poor little head to cause this problem.

When I got to the office (safely, thank goodness), they took me fairly quickly, even though the waiting room was quite full. While the doctor was examining me, I could tell by his manner that this was not a good thing. His first words were to tell me to see a neurologist. Of course I handled this in a mature, calm way – I immediately burst into tears!

They took me to the doctor's private office so I could use the phone (I was scaring the other patients). There I called one of my best friends, also a doctor. She was an OB/GYN, so this wasn't her area of expertise, but I usually got all my doctor referrals from her. She knew who the good doctors were so I knew she could point me in the right direction.

I don't even remember getting home that night or what I said to Steve. I was able to arrange an appointment with a neurologist the next morning. He had me do some strange things, like walk up and down the hallway while he timed me. I didn't know what this had to do with my vision problem. He told me I needed to get an MRI, but didn't think I had a brain tumor – BRAIN TUMOR! I didn't realize that's what he had been considering. So of course I immediately assumed I had a brain tumor and burst into tears again. I had to sweat it out through a long weekend before the test could be scheduled.

I didn't know anything about MRI's. I found out I had to lie still in a very small tube while they took pictures of my brain. I also found out that I was very claustrophobic! The doctor gave me three great tips on getting through having an MRI. They helped me, so I'll share them with you.

1. Close your eyes before they slide you in and keep them closed until you are completely out again.

2. Tuck your thumbs under your bottom so your hands won't touch the sides of the tube.

3. Since my feet are the only things left out during the test, he said my husband should hold onto my ankles and talk to me so I wouldn't feel alone.

All these things really helped. It also helped when he gave me some good drugs to relax before and during the test! Recently I have used "open" MRI's, which helped somewhat with the claustrophobia, but the results aren't always good enough. When I needed a four-hour MRI in a closed tube, I opted for an IV and slept through the whole thing! I admit it - I'm a claustrophobic wimp!

That first MRI was memorable in many ways. The tech doing the testing (it took over two hours) had to stop several times to take care of his two small children. Evidently he was "babysitting" them in the next room. Now, I'm a big supporter of working parents and enjoy small children, but I was in the middle of a major medical crisis here, so give me a break!

The doctor had ordered the test "with contrast" which meant that part way through the test, the tech had to put dye into my blood before taking more pictures. He tried unsuccessfully to find a vein inside both my elbows (major bruises for weeks). Then he said he would find a nurse to do it and left the room. We were in the basement of a very large hospital so this shouldn't have been a problem. However he came back alone, saying he couldn't find anyone, and then said "Oh, you don't need that anyway."

My husband and I made an appointment with the neurologist to review the results. However they postponed it because they didn't have the results yet. Finally we met with him, but he said he was told we took the film with us. News to us! We told him about the babysitting and showed him the bruises on my arms. Turns out he really did want the contrast. After all my trauma, it seems they lost the MRI films!

After talking with my doctor, the head of radiology had what he thought was a very generous solution – I could repeat the tests at no charge. My stress level went off the chart. How could I go through that again?

Fortunately for me, they finally found the films. Have you ever seen the inside of your brain? It's a very strange feeling. Not that I knew what I was looking at, but when the doctor showed me some bright white spots, I knew that wasn't a good sign.

The good news: no sign of a brain tumor. The not-so-good news: those white spots were the plaque (scars) left behind from my body attacking my nervous system. There were multiple spots, so multiple scars = multiple sclerosis. In my case the nerves that had been attacked were the optic nerves, causing the problem with my vision.

Since I had no other symptoms of MS, the neurologist said that I probably wouldn't have other problems, so I shouldn't worry about it. My eye would probably return to normal. What a relief to hear that! He said there weren't any treatments or medications available that I needed to take.

Over the next six months I slowly regained most of the vision in my right eye. I remember being very excited one day because I could finally read the license plate of the car in front of me on the freeway! Those are very large numbers, but when you have MS, you learn to celebrate tiny victories. I suppose you're wondering why I was still driving in that condition. Yes, believe it or not, I was still driving! There was a back-stabbing co-worker after my job, so I didn't dare take off on sick leave right then.

Later I found out that a couple months after seeing me, my doctor quit practicing and went into research (I have that effect on people), so I didn't see another neurologist for five or six years. Unfortunately, I also found out that his advice had not been correct. There definitely were medications I should have been taking that might have slowed down the disease progression and made a big difference in the level of my disability!

During this time, I began having problems with my left knee and had developed a limp which continued to worsen. It is very upsetting to know that some of my problems might have been prevented if I had received better information. I have often wished I could go back to that point in time to do things differently. But all we can do is move forward and make the most of our lives – and get a second opinion about anything important!

That was in the dark ages – before the Internet! Now there is so much more information available to everyone.

Since that time I have gathered a plethora of doctors to help me fight this battle. The following chapters will take you through some of this journey. So come along with me for the ride. *MS is definitely more than a disease – it's an adventure!*

Humpty Dumpty

Several years ago, when I could still stand and walk a little while holding onto things, I went into our laundry room. I reached for the car keys, but my legs began to spasm. As my legs stiffened up, my whole body went straight like a board, causing me to lose my balance. I tried to grab onto anything to keep from falling, but the only thing within reach was the washing machine I was standing next to. Have you ever tried grabbing onto a washer? It was like trying to grab onto a slippery, greased ice cube.

As I felt myself falling backwards, I thought, "Oh, no – my head is going to hit the tile floor!" Well, fortunately that didn't happen. Unfortunately instead, my head hit the edge of a low shelf where we kept shoes. After I hit the floor (and shelf), my body was still so stiff I couldn't move. I reached behind my head to prop it up so I could see. My hand felt wet. I knew this was not a good thing.

It was about 5pm on a Friday afternoon. My family has a policy of only getting hurt or sick after 5pm on Fridays after all the regular doctors' offices have closed. This is especially true on long holiday weekends. We've taken turns to see who can be in the hospital over Thanksgiving weekend. Nothing quite like Thanksgiving turkey from the hospital cafeteria!

My husband and daughter were both home, but in some other part of the house. Our house isn't very big, but they were not within calling range. So I had to just lie there and wait for a couple hours (in my mind – actual time was probably only a few minutes, but I can't remember very clearly). Finally I heard my husband nearby. When he saw me, he got my daughter, and they somehow got me back onto my scooter. Seeing the puddle of blood on the floor almost made me faint. I tried to be very brave so I wouldn't upset them. My husband bandaged up my head as best he could. They managed to get me into the van so he could take me to the nearby hospital emergency room.

Another fun Friday night at the local emergency room. There were only a couple of other people in the waiting room, but it was still an hour or two before they took me into the back. It's amazing all the little corners they have to tuck people into in the emergency room.

It's all still a big blur for me. I remember them taking me to get my head x-rayed. The table was cold and hard. I may have had a CT-scan, too, but I'm not sure. Finally they decided it was time to fix my head. As they began cleaning up my head, all of a sudden I felt very hot and sick to my stomach. I thought, "This is no time for a hot flash!" Someone got my head down before I passed out. They found a fan to blow on me. I think I had started to go into shock.

It took all the king's horses and all the king's men twenty staples to put Humpty Dumpty back together again. The x-ray showed no broken bones. The next few days are a big blur. This was probably from a mild concussion. When I got home, I had to sleep in a recliner for a week or two. I was afraid to stand up or walk – I felt like I would fall backwards again. The walker I had been using helped with balance, but wouldn't protect me from falling backwards. I used my scooter more and more, and walked less and less. This was the beginning of the end of my walking days.

About two weeks later I went to the doctor to have the staples removed. I kept picturing a giant staple remover like the ones I use for paper. I'm not sure what it really looked like, but the pain was excruciating. The nurse decided it was too soon to remove the staples (I was scaring away too many other patients). She also gave me a prescription for some pain medication to put on my head before I came back again.

Since I couldn't see or reach the back of my head, I went an hour before my next appointment so they could put the medicine on my head to help with the pain. Between the medicine and some extra healing time, removing the staples wasn't quite as painful, but certainly not an experience I would recommend to anyone.

The headaches continued for a while (the rocks in my head shift around now and then). My hair hides the big bump and the dent in my head - my souvenirs from this MSAdventure. The next time someone tells me to use my head, *I won't take it literally!*

I Can't Stand it Any More

One of the drugs I use to combat stiffness and spasticity is usually taken orally. Unfortunately, it can have some bad side effects. To help this problem, a clever doctor figured out how to put a small pump filled with the drug under the skin either in the abdomen or the hip area. This has a tube going directly to the spinal fluid where the medicine is needed.

After a test showed that this would work for me, the surgery was scheduled. This took place at a little private hospital in a secluded neighborhood. I felt like someone in the witness protection program for the F.B.I.

The surgery went well (I didn't remember a thing, so I thought it went great!). A few hours later the nurse asked me to try standing by the side of the bed. Can you say, "spaghetti legs"? The medicine in the pump was evidently working all too well. Not only was all the spasticity in my legs gone, so was any control over the muscles.

I thought I would get control back over my legs by the time I went home the next day. Guess again! When we checked out of the hospital, instead of the 200-pound muscular therapist I had seen the day before, the only person available to help my husband get me into the car was a tiny petite nurse. And of course the car was a minivan. It looked like a comedy routine to watch the three of us struggling to get me up and in the van (but we weren't exactly laughing). Having the temperature 91 degrees outside didn't help.

When we got home, I thought it would be simple for me to just slide out of the van onto my little scooter that I use to get around the house. Well my body decided to melt all the way onto the driveway without stopping at the scooter seat. My poor husband had to hoist me back up onto the seat.

Prior to the surgery, I was positive that I had been using my leg muscles to stand. However they said I must have been using the spasticity. I thought the spasticity was interfering with my ability to stand and walk, but instead it must have been helping.

To build up my leg muscles again, I started going to physical therapy a couple of times a week. My legs started getting stronger, but then I maxed out of my physical therapy benefits for the year. I've kept trying to work my legs, but over the last few years the disease progression has been quicker than any muscle building.

I'm very grateful to the people who invented scooters and power wheelchairs, because *I JUST CAN'T STAND IT ANY MORE!*

Backyard Pool Party

Good News: Went out to the pool to go swimming last night.

Bad News: Fell in.

Good News: Did a great somersault getting into the pool.

Bad News: The judge only gave me a 4.2 (she was French).

Good News: I came in first place.

Bad News: I was the only one competing.

Good News: The water felt refreshing.

Bad News: The steps were at that end of the pool.

Good News: The steps are OK.

Bad News: My body protected them.

Good News: Didn't hit my face.

Bad News: My chin and hand were not so lucky.

Good News: No teeth fell out yet.

Bad News: Went under the water.

Good News: My daughter was there to rescue me.

Bad News: She was at the other end of the pool.

Good News: She's a fast swimmer.

Bad News: Not fast enough.

Good News: I survived.

Bad News: My lovely hairdo was ruined.

Good News: I have another MSAdventure to tell you about.

Bad News: I have another MSAdventure to tell you about.

I can't even go in my backyard without having a MSAdventure!

Heat's On

Heat's On

In case you're unsure of how MS works (don't worry, the doctors can't quite figure it out, either), I'll try to explain it in my own words. Note: Please rely on other sources for accurate medical information.

In order for your muscles to work properly, the brain sends a signal through the central nervous system to the muscle with a command, such as "contract" or "relax". The muscle then sends a signal back to the brain with the status of what it's done. This is similar to a lamp with a cord plugged into the wall. The switch will send electricity through the wire to light the lamp.

However if the cord is broken or damaged, the lamp won't light, or will stay lit instead of shutting off. Similarly if the message doesn't get through between the brain and the muscle, the muscle either won't move or won't relax. I'm sure you've seen electrical cords that are frayed or cracked. If the insulation (plastic coating) is damaged, the electrical signal won't go through or may flicker.

Likewise if the protective coating around the nerve (myelin) is damaged, the signal won't connect between the brain and the muscle. MS attacks the myelin sheath around the nerves disrupting the signals to and from the muscles. This can leave a scar (sclerosis) where the damage occurred. If there are several damaged areas there will be many scars or multiple sclerosis.

These scars show up as plaque on MRIs. When my first neurologist showed us the MRI of my brain, there were several bright white spots. As creepy as it was to see slices of my brain, I didn't like seeing those spots – the signs of multiple sclerosis.

Depending on the location and extent of these scars, this can lead to disability. The brain is quite resilient, and can often find alternate pathways around the damaged areas. However the spinal column doesn't have as much room for alternative pathways. My latest MRIs have shown plaque in my spinal column as well. This is likely the cause of my disability.

One environmental factor that can influence the symptoms of MS is the temperature. With MS, heat's the enemy. Getting overheated either from being in high temperatures, a Jacuzzi, or strenuous exercise can affect how your body works. It's much more than just feeling hot. When I get too hot, it sucks the life and energy right out of me. My legs turn to jell-o; I'm like a ragdoll. So where do I live? - Phoenix, Arizona!

I've discovered a whole world of products designed to aid someone with heat issues. There are packs you keep in your freezer and then put on your neck or anywhere you feel hot. Or maybe you prefer the cloths you soak in water then wear as a headband, wristband or around your neck while the water evaporates. For a fashion statement, try a vest with lots of little pockets which hold little ice packs. The selection is endless. There are even machines that have a place to put your hands. This will cool your whole body down.

So stay out of the lovely sunshine (I hibernate in the summer instead of the winter). Select your favorite cool article of clothing. *Find a good book, like "How to Build an Igloo," and hide out until winter – or at least fall.*

Team Sport

So many doctors, so little time to see them all – and so little money to pay them! I used to think that having a Primary Care doctor and an OB/GYN was rather extravagant. Little did I know that this would be just the tip of my future medical iceberg!

I found out quickly that MS is a team sport. Following is an impressive list of specialists who would all join me on this crazy Adventure. I've included a brief description of who they are – in my own terminology. It may not be how it's defined on their business cards, but it's how I see them.

It's so important to find doctors who are both competent and easy for you to talk to. Don't hesitate to find someone new if your needs aren't being met.

Primary Care Physician (PCP) – the ringmaster of this circus; my main support through all my physical challenges. She listens to my hypochondriac ravings and sorts through to the concerns that we need to do something about. If she can't resolve an issue herself, she will recommend other additions to my team of doctors and follow up afterwards.

OB/GYN – essential for all women. Mine is one of my best friends outside the office as well. She's had me in the operating room four times and I'm still here! Once was to assist in removing my gall bladder – the ugliest baby she ever delivered!

Neurologist – my main MS expert. It may take a few tries to find a doctor who understands both MS and your private battle. Find someone you can talk with easily and who takes an active role in your treatment. I finally found a wonderful one, but then she deserted me and moved to the dark side – joined a drug company! Fortunately I found a new one that is smart and caring. This is a critical doctor for those fighting the MS battle.

Neurosurgeon – installed the pump that puts a drug directly into my spinal fluid, thus avoiding systemic (cool word – it means system-wide or overall body) side effects, like fatigue, which I get more than my share of anyway.

Ophthalmologist – saved my eyesight when nasty bacteria tried to eat a hole through my cornea. Always has an encouraging smile.

Optometrist – created designer glasses for me when the cornea-eating bacteria left me with double vision in one eye.

Physiatrist – fancy title for rehab doctor. She directs my physical therapy and also is my pump doctor for my intrathecal pump, monitoring and adjusting the flow and refilling as needed.

Dermatologist – known to us as Dr. Freeze – she always enters the exam room armed with her canister of chemicals ready to freeze off any signs of sun damage. Since I'm a redhead who grew up before sun block, there's always something to target. Whenever I go to the skin doctor I look like I've come down with the measles.

Hormone specialist – after I had a hysterectomy, I suffered for several years from hormonal imbalance (not fun for either me or those around me). Finally found a doctor who specialized in bio-identical hormone therapy. This was a small miracle for me until I got a DVT (deep vein thrombosis – a blood clot in my leg). This was probably caused from spending too much time sitting in a wheelchair instead of walking around (like I had a choice!). But just in case the cause was my hormone therapy, my PCP wouldn't let me take estrogen any more. Fortunately my hormone doctor had other alternatives and believes in vitamins, so he's added an important level of health care to my routine.

Hematologist – added to my list to deal with the DVT. Now I'm on blood thinner medication that has to be continually monitored by the vampires who jab my finger every 2-4 weeks.

Podiatrist – once I stopped using my feet for walking, I mistakenly thought I wouldn't need a foot doctor any more. Now, however, I need her even more to help with trimming the toe nails that I can't reach, fixing the damage that I do to my toes from banging them as I get off and on my scooter, dealing with the pressure sore on my ankle bone from sleeping on my side, treating the swelling from edema, etc.

Physical Therapist (P.T.) – lovingly known as Primary Torturer. He cruelly enjoys forcing my legs to straighten out – they only want to stay in a sitting position.

Occupational Therapist (O.T.) – takes charge of the upper body. When my hands first started cramping up, I panicked. Fortunately my O.T. developed a hand exercise program which gave me back the use of my left hand.

P.T. Edema Specialist – massaged and bandaged my swollen feet and ankles to reduce the swelling caused by gravity and lack of use of my leg muscles.

Speech Therapist – tested my swallowing technique (see "Tough Act to Swallow"), helped with voice problems, and saved me from the feeding tube.

Massage Therapist – the only time my legs and the rest of my body feel at all relaxed and comfortable is when I'm on the massage table. I need to be there for an hour and a half instead of the usual hour, because my body's such a mess it takes that long for her to deal with all the tightness and knots. The time passes so quickly when it hurts so good!

Respiratory Therapist – helped me conquer horrible pneumonia.

Urologist – when they used a catheter in the hospital, my body forgot how to work. Some new medicine helped straighten me out.

Gastroenterologist – MS can affect the insides, too. She's everyone's favorite colonoscopy specialist (dirty job, but someone's got to do it). The prep is the worst part. Thanks to the IV medications, I don't remember the rest.

Dentist – been through a lot together. Even though most are capped, I still have all my own teeth (except my I.Q. dropped when they removed my wisdom teeth).

Psychiatrist – never thought I'd need one of these, but he helps me handle the stresses brought on by both the disease and the treatments.

Counselor – she works together with my psychiatrist. Her suggestions help me deal with my challenges. Search till you find someone with a positive outlook that you really connect with – you don't have to go it alone. Heidi's laughter puts me at ease. Our talks lighten my load.

Neuropsychologist – extra-special help for us extra-special people (see "Dr. Midnight").

ENT – ear, nose and throat specialist. I've seen this doctor for various sinus and ear infections over the years. It seems MS is now trying to stop me from saying bad things about it by stealing my voice. So the ENT put a camera down my nose into my throat (not the most fun procedure) to look at my vocal chords. They looked perfect, which means MS is probably the culprit attacking the nerves that control my voice.

Botox – I've been having Botox injections for the last year – no, not because I'm vain and want a plastic face. The spasms in my legs cause my knees to lock together. The Botox helps my legs relax a little. Do my legs look 10 years younger now?

Oral facial myologist – this was actually one of my daughter's doctors that taught her how to swallow differently to cure her tongue thrust problem. I just added it to the list because I think it's a cool title!

And the list goes on. Some doctors I won't need to see any more (we can only hope – nothing personal, docs), while others will be added to my list as needed. I'm grateful for the help I've received from all these smart and caring people.

Each of us will have our own list. *MS is nasty, so be sure to get the help you need in your life.*

Wake-up Call

This is an email I wrote to a friend about five years ago.

My MSAdventures start before I even wake up! This morning I woke up about 5am with pain in my foot. It had slipped off the bed and was caught between the bed and the metal arm on my scooter. This was causing my foot to spasm about every two seconds against the sharp metal. Not a nice way to wake up.

I tried to get up, but couldn't move that foot, and the other one was pinned under it. I couldn't sit up, because my legs were pinned sideways. I couldn't move the scooter because it was plugged into the charger. I didn't want to wake my husband up because he needed his sleep for work. And as if that wasn't bad enough, the worst part was that I very badly needed a trip to the bathroom!

I finally managed to pull out the charging cord from my scooter so I could move it enough to get my feet out. Somehow I managed to pull myself onto the scooter.

I knew I couldn't make it to the larger hall bath in time, so I tried for the tiny bathroom closer by. However, in my hurry, the curtain covering the archway in between the bedroom and the bathroom got caught on the scooter. The curtain came crashing down on top of me, breaking the rod. After extricating myself from the curtain, I finally made it into the tiny bathroom – a little too late, of course. Now you probably need a trip there from laughing so hard at my trauma!

The only way I could get through it all was by thinking about telling you. *Got to laugh, right?*

P.S. My husband never woke up – I knew he needed his sleep!

Changes in Latitude, Changes in Attitude

All you "parrot heads" will recognize these words from the Jimmy Buffet song. For those non-feathered friends, this song is about the way his attitude changes when he changes latitude, which he does by going down south to the islands. I'm sure spending a little time in Margarita-ville doesn't hurt the attitude changes either, although getting a cheeseburger in Paradise is more my style.

Those of us who can't get away to the Caribbean right now but still need an attitude adjustment will need to find another method. Last year I took a great Bible study class called, "The Frazzled Female." Sound like anyone you know? This class was about ways to handle all the stresses in life. One topic was about changing your attitude or way of looking at a situation.

As a reminder of this concept, we all were given little red ponytail holders – a small elastic band – to wear on our wrists. Whenever we recognized a negative attitude about something, we were to snap the band to remind us to change our attitude by looking at things differently.

One day while I was taking one of my marathon bus rides trying to get home from a doctor's appointment, I looked up to see where we were, which was about 6 miles from my house. I thought, "Oh, no – we're only as far as Camelback Road." This made the ride seem endless.

Then I happened to glance down at my wrist and saw the band. I snapped it – amazing how a little pain can trigger behavior modification! I tried to think of a way to change my attitude. Instead of my previous statement, I thought, "Wow! We're all the way to Camelback Road already!" – you know, the glass half full, not half empty.

It surprised me how much better I felt. The ride didn't seem interminable any more. My thoughts became more positive and cheerful. Before I realized it, the bus was pulling in front of my house to drop me off.

Although it was quite the fashion statement, I don't wear the little band any more. Now that the bruises on my wrist have finally faded, I still try to remember this lesson whenever I find myself in a negative zone. You can't always change the situation you're in, but whether you think so or not, you CAN change your way of looking at it. Sometimes it can be a real challenge, but definitely worth the effort. I often think of how I'll tell my email buddy, Lu Ann, about the current situation so we can laugh about it. That helps me be more creative and positive.

If you're having a problem with a negative attitude, try the rubber band trick – easy on the snapping, though. It's supposed to be a reminder, not punishment! It can also help to take a little trip to the islands, if only in your mind, or to whatever fills your mind with positive vibes. *A little trip to Margarita-ville or a cheeseburger from McDonald's could help, too!*

An Aisle Too Far

On one of my trips from the doctor's office, I took the opportunity to stop at the grocery store. I knew I was running out of time before the bus came to pick me up. I just needed one more item. This ended up being in a far corner of the store. I thought I could make it there and back in time. Of course, when I found what I was looking for, where else would it be but on the top shelf – and no one in sight to reach it for me.

The wheelchair I had that day was equipped with a power lift option, which will lift me up about six inches. Fortunately this was just enough to reach what I needed. Unfortunately my battery was running low – using this lift option evidently took a little too much juice. When I started to hurry back to the checkout counter, my wheelchair would not hurry – it would only blink at me!

Now I was really stuck. I knew the bus driver would be pulling up any moment. Finally I saw a young woman sweeping the floor way down the long aisle. After waving like a crazy person for a little while, she finally saw me and came over (brave soul!). I explained to Cathy that my battery had died, and asked her if she would push me back to the front of the store.

She was quite willing to help me – I guess it beat sweeping the floor. However before this could happen, I had to take the chair out of gear. This was a fairly new chair for me. I knew the switch for the gears was in front on the bottom near my feet. I knew this because when I first got the chair, I kept accidentally bumping the switch with my heels and shutting down the chair! So my husband had wedged in a block of Styrofoam so this would not happen.

Now I had to explain to Cathy how to undo this. It was too awkward for me to reach myself. She wasn't able to do it, so she walked away quickly. I started to panic as I heard my name being paged, calling me to the front of the store. All I could do was sit helplessly feeling deserted. Soon Cathy came back with a big guy co-worker. He was able to get the Styrofoam out, and after several tries, they got the levers switched the right way to take the chair out of gear.

Cathy was fairly small, and the chair is quite big, so I thought the big guy would offer to push me. But he took off right away. Nice little Cathy proceeded to push my chair down the long aisle to the front. Since I had several grocery items balanced on my lap all this time, she took me through the self-check aisle and helped me check out. We then went out to the front door where, fortunately, my bus driver had waited for me. It happened to be Chris, one of my favorite drivers. He said he knew I was in the store somewhere.

Chris took over the pushing job from wonderful Cathy. When I got home, I called the store and told the manager how awesome she had treated me. I hope she got some sort of helpful employee award. Meanwhile, Chris had to push me onto the lift and get me strapped into the bus. When we got to my house, he had to get me out of the bus, push me up the ramp into my house, and help me onto my little scooter that I use inside.

We ended up having to replace the batteries in the chair. I'm so thankful there are people like Cathy and Chris that are willing to go out of their way to help a person in a wheelchair who has been stranded *an aisle too far.*

Jumping Jacks

So what's the deal? – When I want to move my legs or feet they won't move. Then when I would like to just relax, my legs want to do jumping jacks. Is that fair?

One of the joys of dealing with spasticity is clonus. Clonus (from the Greek for "violent, confused motion") is a series of involuntary muscular contractions due to sudden stretching of the muscle. The result is the rapid bouncing or jerking of the leg. When I complained about this to my neurologist one day, she said, "It's only cosmetic." Her tone of voice was quite unsympathetic. She obviously didn't consider this side effect to be worth discussing. I agree that this uncontrollable bouncing of the foot and leg are not life-threatening – but it sure can be annoying and embarrassing!

Clonus seems to be caused when a nerve gets irritated. Since I have a lot of nerve (or so I've been told), I get attacks of clonus frequently. One thing that will always start my foot going is to pull up on the ball of my foot. This will set my foot to tapping and my lower leg bouncing. The doctors do this occasionally to test my spasticity – one test I don't have to worry about passing – without even studying!

This can also happen from moving my foot to a different spot or position. Frequently this occurs while I'm at the gym – the Adapted Fitness Center. As I move from machine to machine, the assistant needs to move my feet to different positions or back and forth between my wheelchair and the current piece of exercise equipment. The problem happens when my foot is set down. If it's set down too hard or in a weird position, this will trigger the clonus. My foot will start bouncing up and down rapidly. At first I was sometimes able to stop it by bending my foot to push down on my toes, but as my muscles have gotten weaker and less responsive, this will not work any more.

For most people, the standard remedy is to push down on the knee. This pressure will be transmitted to the foot, thus stopping the tremors. Of course my body has to be different. Pushing down on my knee is the worst thing to do – it causes the jumping to get increasingly worse.

The only thing I've found that will work for me is to lift up my leg just behind the knee, then gently set the foot back down. However, lifting my leg is always a challenge. It takes both of my hands and some leverage from an armrest to lift my leg and hold it for a few seconds until my foot stops moving. If both feet get into the act, I will try to deal with one at a time, but often it takes lifting both legs for the activity to cease.

I've tried to teach others what to do, with limited success. Some people just have the knack for it, while others can't quite do it right, or undo it by setting my foot down wrong, triggering even worse bouncing. Andy, who is in charge of the Adapted Fitness Center, has the "magic touch". Sometimes the other assistants will call him over for help when their efforts are just making matters worse. Andy is able to calm my legs down almost instantly.

One of the machines I use in the Adapted Fitness Center is the "flexercisor." This has pedals similar to a bicycle with long handles that move back and forth for my arms while the pedals turn. My feet are strapped onto the pedals with a Velcro strap. My right foot is known to slip out of my shoe, so it is further strapped on with another long Velcro strap. My legs are also strapped on individually to pull my knees out to the sides because my thigh muscles constantly pull them together. (Please don't pull the fire alarm – I'm obviously not going anywhere even though I'm riding a bicycle!)

Finally the pedals are moving and the handles are going back and forth. All seems well, when all of a sudden the clonus monster takes over, causing my legs to try to bounce around. Remember, they are all strapped down. They try to move anyway, causing the machine to bang loudly like it's being shaken apart (not too comfortable for me, either). Of course this causes everyone to stare at me, something I just adore. I can usually lift up enough on my legs to stop the jumping. Sometimes I have to stop the machine, fix my legs, and then start it up again. If Andy or an assistant is standing nearby, they will stop the machine and try to help. When the excitement is over for the moment, I continue on with my ride. This may happen several times during my twenty minutes on that machine.

The neurologist said that twenty minutes of exercising might be too long, fatiguing the muscles. But it's the only leg exercise I do all week, so I don't want to give it up or cut it short. Sigh.

Another movement that will cause a similar problem is when my legs are bumped or jarred, such as when I'm in my wheelchair and roll over a bump. And the bumps in life are everywhere!

The thresholds of many doorways often trigger the spasms. What a wonderful way to enter a room. Per Murphy's Law, these doorways will be going into places that are full of people, such as busy stores or quiet doctor's offices where the noise of my jumping feet echo around. There will typically be no room to pull my wheelchair out of the way so I can take the time and effort to get my poor legs to calm down.

Another place this happens is when I'm going in/out of an elevator. Most people just step right through, but these openings can be quite jarring. Nothing like being trapped in a crowded elevator with my feet bouncing wildly around!

This also frequently occurs when I'm riding in the car, or especially in a bus. The handicapped bus is a wonderful lifesaver, but not exactly known for its smooth ride. Any big bump will trigger a reaction. I can usually get it under control, but the bus driver has been known to stop the bus till I can sit still.

Often when the physical therapist is working on me, he will stretch a muscle a bit too far or move it a certain way and the fun will start. He always wants to know if I'm asking him to dance. I wish I could do other steps besides "the clonus".

Sometimes the clonus can be triggered by a simple stretch or by leaning or reaching a certain way. Other times it is triggered by nothing at all! I'll be sitting there, minding my own business, when my legs start jumping. I can't stop doing what's causing the problem if I'm not doing anything to cause it. MS can certainly be a frustrating disease.

But why am I making such a big deal about this? It's not life-threatening - unless my feet bounce off my scooter in the middle of crossing a busy road (which has happened). After all, *it's "only cosmetic"!*

Murphy's Law MS Version

I've never actually seen it in writing, and I don't know who this person Murphy was, but this is what I've heard is Murphy's Law – "Anything that CAN go wrong, WILL go wrong."

I'd like to make some additional rules for the MS Version:

If an object CAN fall on the floor, it WILL.

When it falls:

- If it's breakable, it will break – in as many pieces as possible.

- If it can roll, it will roll as far away as possible, probably underneath something so it's impossible to reach, even with a little grabber.

- If it's sticky or gooey, it will land with the sticky side down – onto whatever is hardest to clean.

When eating Spaghetti sauce:

- It will splash on whichever piece of clothing is newest or the hardest to clean

- A new white shirt always acts as a spaghetti sauce magnet.

When trying to maneuver down an aisle, especially in a store:

- Everyone else will be trying to go down the same aisle, most likely in the opposite direction.

- Unless you need help – then no one will be anywhere around.

If you need something on a shelf:

- It will be too high to reach, and again, no one will be anywhere around.

- If it's too high it will also be breakable.

- It will also be too heavy to use the little grabber tool.

When waiting for the bus to pick you up:

If you are ready early:

- the bus will be at least ten minutes late.

- the office will be closed because you came too early.

If you are running late:

- the bus will be early.

- you will need to use the bathroom.

- someone will be ringing the doorbell.

- the phone will ring incessantly.

- traffic will be congested.

- the bus will be full of people who will need to get off first.

Don't think, *"Can anything else go wrong?"*, *because the answer is definitely, "Yes!"*

Oh, My Aching Feet

One of the wonderful side effects of buzzing around in a wheelchair instead of walking is edema. This is the condition where your body retains water. In my case for once it's not all in my head – rather it's in my feet! My poor little feet and ankles are so swollen I don't even recognize them any more.

This seems to be a problem with circulation, specifically the lymphatic system. When I could move my legs by walking or any other type of exercise, the fluid in my feet and legs would be carried away by the lymph system. Without the contracting/relaxing of my leg muscles, the fluid builds up.

On top of that is our old buddy – gravity. My doctors keep telling me to keep my feet up to counteract the effects of gravity. Easier said than done. First of all, I physically can't lift my feet up any more. My legs are so stiff and full of spasms that they each feel like they weigh 500 pounds. And they won't bend. Now I've been working with my weights to build up my arm strength, but not enough to lift legs that don't want to move.

The next problem with having my feet up is that it's very hard to do anything in that position, such as getting something to eat or drink, paying bills, doing dishes or laundry, using the bathroom, or most of the many things I need to do all day. Although it sounds like a good thing to just put my feet up, relax, and watch TV, I need help to get there and once I'm there, I'm stuck.

Shoes are a definite problem. I used to wear a size 8 regular. Now even a size 10 double wide won't go on my feet! I ordered four pairs of shoes from a handicapped catalog (never order shoes from a catalog!). Only one fit – these were designed with a wide toe-box (I didn't know shoes had one) especially for edema patients. They actually fit quite well. Too bad they were bright pink fur-lined slippers – not exactly fancy evening wear.

Living in Phoenix, shoes are non-essential while I'm in my wheelchair – except at the gym. There I'm required to wear tennis shoes to use some of the machines. My good friend Judy found some wide men's shoes with Velcro closers. She had to do some minor surgery on them to make the toe box wide enough (now I've learned the correct terminology for that part of a shoe). It takes some effort to stuff my feet into them, but it's usually barely possible. On one exercise machine they have to wrap a wide Velcro strap around my right foot or the foot comes out of the shoe. Occasionally when that happens, the head of the gym says, "Oh, a flat tire." Thank goodness I only need to wear those shoes once or twice a week.

To help with this problem of swollen feet, they recommend "ted" hose. These are lovely fashion-setting stockings that have varying degrees of compression. Basically they are very tight socks that are designed to squeeze the fluid out of your feet upwards. They come in knee high or thigh high. I've seen them in black, white and beige. It takes a magician or a body builder to get them on. Wearing them will keep you very warm and toasty if you live in a cold climate – severely hot and claustrophobic if you're in a hot climate like Phoenix.

Other options include a boot you pull on or tennis shoes tied tightly. They even make little machines that move your feet around or squeeze your legs.

For two weeks I went to a lymphodema therapist. Each day she would do a lymph massage – very light touch on the lymph drainage nodes in the throat, chest, abdomen, down the legs to the feet, and back up again. To me this felt very strange and somewhat ticklish, but with my poor swollen feet I had to try everything.

After that she would wrap my legs from my feet up to my knees. First came a "stockingette" – a thin, stretchy sleeve of white cotton, covering from my toes (open) to my knees. Then she would wrap cotton batting around for cushioning. Next came what looked like ace bandages. These were a special short-stretch version that she wrapped in a special way from my toes to my knees, held in place by masking tape. The final layer was another white stockingette. My legs now looked white and thick. I felt like I had plaster casts on them. So when anyone mentioned anything about them, I calmly explained that I had been in a skiing accident (even though I can't walk and it was 110 degrees outside!).

My legs had to stay mummified until 2 hours before my appointment the next day, when the entire process would be repeated. After two weeks my feet looked considerably more like feet instead of weird shaped balloons. However, once I stopped being gift-wrapped every day, it didn't take long for my feet to puff out again. It's "cooled down" to 104 degrees now, so I try to put up with the ted hose when I can find someone willing to fight with putting them on. It's a good thing I only have to deal with shoes once a week for the gym. *Manolo Blahnik (high fashion shoe designer) won't be getting any business from me!*

If the Shoe Fits

Having puffy feet has caused several additional problems besides the swelling from fluid retention. My right foot started turning outward, causing it to get a pressure sore on the edge of the ball of my foot. To alleviate this situation, as well as find some shoes that would fit my foot, the podiatrist sent me to a company that deals with specialized shoes and other supplies.

When I met Dave at their office, he brought out a shoe with a strap across the top of the foot that closed with Velcro. This made it totally adjustable, even for my oversized foot. After he fit my foot with a shoe of the correct length, Dave surprised us by pulling out the insole.

This exposed the sole of the shoe. Instead of being a solid piece of material, it was made up of many small pieces, similar to a jigsaw puzzle. Dave proceeded to pull out 6-7 little pieces in the area where my sore would press down. When the insole was replaced, this area would no longer cause pressure on that part of my foot.

I was still concerned about the shoe pressing on my puffy toes, but Dave solved this by pulling off the toe section. This left just the wide strap made of soft, black material going across the foot. For a corrective, orthopedic shoe, it was amazingly dressy and attractive.

I thought my shoe challenges were over. I was looking forward to wearing my new pair of shoes, until I found a critical problem – there was only one shoe! Dave explained that the insurance company would only cover the shoe for the foot with the problem.

So much for my new pair of shoes. I tried to explain that both feet were too swollen to fit into regular shoes. In addition, the left foot also had a pressure sore on the heel. Dave said he would need to call the doctor who would have to justify this to the insurance company. This occurred in November. My lonely shoe found its home in the closet.

In January I received a message to call the orthopedic shoe store. I assumed they were calling about payment of the bill. To my surprise, my other shoe was ready to be picked up. Unfortunately I was in the hospital with severe pneumonia, so I explained that I couldn't come in at that time. They agreed to hold it for a while.

After two weeks in the hospital, I was transferred to a rehab facility. There I stayed for over four weeks trying to get my strength back. I still wasn't able to take care of myself at home, so next I went to a group home. When I called the store to tell them I still wasn't able to pick up the shoe, they suggested that someone stop by to deliver it.

In a few days Dave came by to fit the other shoe to my left foot. The ironic thing is that now that I might finally get my special shoes to fit my poor swollen feet, all the lying in bed and medication had helped my feet return to almost normal size. Of course the new shoe fit with no problem. He again took some jigsaw pieces out of the sole to relieve the pressure on my heel.

So did I finally have a well-fitting pair of shoes to wear? Unfortunately "No," the first shoe was still at home safely tucked away in the closet somewhere. When that one is found and brought over to the group home, the answer will finally be, "Yes". *So if the shoe fits, wear it!*

Useless words

For those of us who are "mobility-challenged" (stuck in a wheelchair), some words or phrases have lost their meaning. Sometimes when I am in a really bad mood and feeling sorry for myself, it irritates me to think how thoughtless and insensitive other people are to use these words around me. Then I think about it and have to just laugh or smile to myself.

Now and then, if they're lucky, I give others the privilege of hearing one of my witty, clever, sarcastic remarks about what they just said. Usually I keep those remarks to myself and just chuckle on the inside. I'm sure this is the best way since I'm usually the only one who finds my remarks humorous.

This is a list of some of those useless words and phrases:

"Walk right in"

If only I could

"Walk this way"

Oh, how I wish I could

"Have a seat/take a seat"

No thanks, brought my own

"Sit down, please"

Already sitting

"Sit down and make yourself comfortable"

Already sitting, never comfortable

"Standing room only"

Guess that let's me out

"Run to the store"

Where are my jogging shoes?

"Run and get something"

I'll "roll" over, is that OK?

"Run over to ..."

This phrase can be used for multiple occasions,

none of which will find me "running".

And finally, one of my favorites:

"Just relax"

This is what my physical therapist says as he's stretching and trying to straighten my legs. If I could relax, I wouldn't need him any more – he'd be out of a job!

Actually I have found some advantages to not being able to follow these requests:

For those shy people who'd rather not be noticed:

"Will all the newcomers stand up?"

If you are self-conscious about your age:

"All people over 40 step forward."

Don't like to talk or be recognized in front of a group:

"Please come up on the stage when your name is called."

Sorry, there isn't a ramp!

I notice more of these phrases all the time. Instead of letting them get me down, I mentally add them to the list, and see what clever, witty remark I can think up. Fortunately for everyone, I usually keep them to myself – and *let everyone wonder what I am grinning about!*

Rehab and Other Fun Vacation Spots

Dr. Midnight

Once when I was in the rehab hospital, my case worker recommended that I talk with a neuropsychologist. I had no idea what this type of doctor would do for me, but I was willing to try. However, she was an elusive doctor to find. Finally one night around 10pm (very late for most people in rehab except for those who can't sleep, like me), the nurse told me that the doctor would be in soon.

I had assumed she was a doctor at the hospital, but evidently she didn't have an office there. Since it was so late, we had to find a place to meet. The first time we went to the empty waiting room by the main entrance, which was now dark and deserted. This was in a corner of the hospital far from the patient rooms.

The doctor sat on the couch with her clipboard and papers while I was in my little scooter. She proceeded to ask me a million questions about my personal information, my medical history, etc., - all the boring stuff that goes on forms for a new patient. Shortly after we started talking, my intestines began feeling upset and began to cramp. I tried to ignore this and keep answering the questions. Finally I had to tell her I wasn't feeling well.

I felt an urgent need to get back to my bathroom, so I told her I had to leave. However she was determined to complete her paperwork. So as I started in a panic to ride my scooter as fast as it would go down the dark hallways back to my room, the doctor ran alongside me with her clipboard in hand, continuing to ask me questions. My mind was focused on trying to get to my bathroom in time, so I don't know what I answered. I'm sure I was making no sense at all. We had to be quite a sight rushing down that hallway.

It was quite a distance to my room, but thankfully I made it just in time. A minute later the bathroom door opened, and there was the doctor, still with her clipboard in her hand. (See chapter on Privacy in rehab.) I finally told her I couldn't answer any more questions that night. (some people just can't take a hint)

After that night, we met several more times, whenever I could find the phantom doctor - always after dark when everyone else was asleep. We would meet either in an empty lounge area or often in the dark spooky cafeteria. In the morning I would wonder if I really met with her or if it had just been a dream in the night.

Coping with rehab was a continuing problem. When the doctor asked how I coped with things outside of rehab, I mentioned writing this book to try to keep my sense of humor. She suggested that I write about rehab the same way. I told her if I did, there would be a chapter about her. I still picture us like some cartoon characters with me racing to the bathroom in a panic on my little red scooter and the phantom doctor running alongside me with her clipboard. Well, doc, you helped me survive and laugh about rehab, so *this chapter's for you!*

Roommates

Some roommates can be fun and stay your friend for life (like Arlene, my college roommate). Others can be obnoxious or, in the worst case, can be hazardous to your health!

When I went to the rehab hospital the first time, I had a variety of roommates. To start with, I had the best roommate – no one! Soon someone arrived in the middle of the night, along with an entourage of noisy doctors, nurses and family members. The machines that were connected to her were even noisy. I hoped these were just "moving in" sounds, but the chaos continued the next day and evening. Did I mention that the patient herself was loud, demanding and whiny?

Out of self-preservation, I spent all my time when I should have been in my room resting, in the puzzle room looking for pieces of a cloud or a barn that I'm sure had been lost long ago. The nurses took pity on me and convinced the doctor to move my roommate to another room. Finally I had peace and quiet in my room, but you'll never guess what happened next.

Evidently Ms. Whiny didn't know she was moved out so she would be away from me. Suddenly she became my best buddy (in her mind only). At every meal she would find my table. At therapy sessions she would find me. Even in the hallways she would be next to me. I guess she missed me!

Another time when I went to rehab I had to play musical rooms. My first roommate had loud phone conversations all night long – in her sleep! The next one snored so loud no one could sleep. I switched rooms so I could get the window bed.

Unfortunately the next roommate they moved in was the worst. This one should have been sent to a regular hospital instead of rehab. For the first two days she was sick to her stomach and coughed horribly night and day. I hid out in the puzzle room out of self defense! She never went to therapy, which was, I thought, the whole purpose of that hospital. I tried to tell them that I was there this time because I had just had an IV infusion of medicine to knock out my immune system. This meant I was susceptible to everything. My new roommate was making me sick. But no one would listen.

By Friday night, my roomie had the place all to her coughing self because I was in an ambulance being transferred to the hospital where I spent the next week trying to recover from severe pneumonia. I found out later that I should have contacted my neurologist. She would have done something about the situation.

After a horrible week in the hospital wondering if I would survive, I was shipped back to the rehab hospital for two and a half more weeks to try to get some strength back after the pneumonia. My hospital stay had been a giant setback to say the least. I was still on oxygen, and felt like a ragdoll. Fortunately my next roomie was wonderfully blah – no major issues. I was just beginning to benefit from the physical therapy when I was sent home.

The very next day started the happy events surrounding my daughter's graduation from college. Fortunately my sister, Jane, came to help me or I couldn't have made it to all the functions. I was so grateful to be out of the hospital and rehab in time to see my daughter wear her cap & gown. My friends had brought two lovely new outfits for me to wear. It was a wonderful family time. A beautiful family picture sits in my home today of that special occasion that I almost missed.

So beware of roommates. I'll take the one "on the phone" all night next time!

Therapy Buddies

When I was first sent to the rehabilitation hospital, I wasn't sure how long I would be there. The intent was for me to get some good physical therapy while regulating my pump medication. This is the medication used to control spasticity. The pump is surgically implanted either into the abdomen or, in my case, into the hip area. The medication is dispersed in the fluid that bathes the spinal cord to avoid the side effects to my system from taking it orally. It is regulated by a "magic" control that the doctor puts over the pump area. The signal goes through my skin to communicate with the pump. It can be told how much medicine to inject and when. It also reports back to let the doctor know how much medicine is left.

One feature I haven't tested out yet is the alarm that goes off when the pump is low. Whenever I have the pump refilled, it gives an alarm date. I schedule my next refill date to occur before I start beeping. I've come close, but have never experienced the alarm.

Back to rehab. I'm a very shy, quiet person, especially around people I don't know. When I went to rehab, I naturally thought I would just keep to myself and concentrate on my therapy. Most patients were recovering from some type of surgery, such as knee or hip replacements or shoulder repairs or even heart bypass surgery. Most were quite a bit older than me. They all seemed a bit strange to me (hence the term "strangers"), as I'm sure I did to them. I would never have believed that some of them would become close friends.

For meals, everyone ate in a cafeteria. At my first meal, I happened to sit next to Margaret. There were about 6-8 people at the table in various stages of recovery. Naturally I learned way more than I needed or wanted to know about everyone's surgery, diseases, and bodily functions. Did I mention my lack of appetite?

It was very competitive to see who had the worst operation, the toughest therapist, the fewest visitors – even an age contest. One lady was bragging about being 81 years old. Not to be outdone, another jumped in to say, "Well, I just turned 90!" For a non-alcoholic cafeteria, there was an awful lot of "whine" at the table. I thought how little I had in common with all these people – and how long this hospital stay was going to be.

As I went back to my room, it turned out that Margaret was my next-door neighbor. Since she had just come the day before, she didn't know anyone either, so we planned on meeting for dinner. Her roommate was very outgoing and friendly. We talked at dinner about not wanting to sit at a table with whiny, negative people. So we tried to be positive and happy and friendly. It must have been contagious, for soon we had our own group of regulars. We even did the unthinkable – laughed a lot. Other people tried to join our table, which was OK, but it was a "no-whine" zone. I told Jan, an old high-school buddy, about the group, and she said, "Oh, you're at the popular table."

These women became my therapy family. They referred to me as the teenager of the table (I was only in my fifties!). We all looked out for each other. One of the women knew everything about everyone, including the personal lives of all the staff – but in a good, caring way, not gossipy. If anyone missed a meal, or was having a tough day, the rest of us did whatever we could to help. For a shy loner, I was amazed at how much these women meant to me – so quickly.

After about a week and a half, most people completed their therapy and made a break for the outside world. It turned out that I stayed for over three weeks, so soon my therapy buddies all left – I was devastated. Margaret had become especially close, so she promised to call me. True to her word, she called every day while I was in rehab. She even called after I went home, and has continued to call every day since – and that was more than 5 years ago!

Isn't it a great feeling, no matter how the day has gone, to know that someone cares enough to call? *You never know where or when you will meet a friend.*

Privacy

If you're looking for privacy at the rehab hospital, you'd better pack a dictionary in your suitcase, because that's the only place you'll find it!

Usually a closed door means, "keep out" or "go away – I'm busy doing something private and don't want to be disturbed right now." However at the rehab hospital a closed door means something more like "come on in, everyone, and see what embarrassing thing I'm doing."

The first day when I had the audacity to close my bathroom door, the occupational therapist barged in like it was normal to do so. She had come to remind me that I had a therapy appointment in five minutes.

I thought she was rather rude and insensitive to barge in like that. However I was soon to find out that this was the norm here – and the more people the merrier! I began to think that my bathroom was the party room for the hospital. Doctors, nurses, therapists, other patients and their families all began flocking to my bathroom.

Other patients' kids were particularly welcome, because they didn't hesitate to ask questions or make comments about the situation.

This was especially true the day when three or four nurses, aides, and others were trying to insert a catheter into my bladder. It was a Sunday afternoon. I was in my own hospital room on my bed. They were trying unsuccessfully to complete the embarrassing procedure. Additional staff came to try periodically. I was on my bed with the curtain between the beds drawn and the door shut – we all know what that means. At first my roommate was gone, but soon came back to the room – with her whole family! Little kids kept trying to peak around the curtain to see what was going on.

Outside my window was a courtyard. Since it was a sunny Sunday afternoon, there were lots of people walking around. I asked the nurse to close the blinds so I wouldn't be putting on a show for everyone, but she said no one could see in the window. Of course I found out later how wrong she was, but I wasn't in any position to do anything about it. Since it was taking so long, my physical therapist came by to see why I was late to my next appointment. I begged them not to let him in. He kept coming back every 5-10 minutes.

Finally someone came that knew what they were doing and finished the procedure. By then my roommate and her family had gone, it was getting dark so all the visitors outside were leaving, and I had missed my whole physical therapy appointment. I was exhausted from all the stress and trauma.

Just another bright, sunny, relaxing Sunday afternoon at rehab.

Noah, Where's Your Ark?

While in rehab, I experienced three great floods.

The first occurred during shower time. I was really enjoying the shower when the nurse came running in from the hallway shouting for me to stop. I couldn't see anything wrong but evidently the way I had braced the sprayer handle against the shower chair was forcing the water through some hidden crack in the tile - it was flooding the hallway right through the wall!

Another time I dared to take a shower, the washcloth unknowingly fell onto the floor, thus blocking the drain. The water began overflowing the shower stall, gushing out through the bathroom doorway, flooding the tiny space in front of the closet, sneaking out under the room door, and yes, once again, gushing out into the hallway.

Needless to say, from that point on, they watched closely whenever I took a shower – an awkward situation for me to say the least!

Then one morning I woke up to hear the nurse open the door. As she approached my bed, I heard her shoes go, "slosh, slosh, slosh!" The strange sound grew louder as she came closer. When she rounded the end of the bed to the side, the explanation for the sound became all too clear – evidently the nurses the night before had neglected to close the valve on the bag connected to my bladder. So gross!

While the nurse was concerned about her soggy shoes and how to clean up the mess, I was worrying about all my clothes, books and other stuff that had probably been left on the floor and was now ruined. Luckily most of my things had been put away or were up on the counter or the chair.

However, the one thing that had been left standing on its side on the floor leaning against the chair was my brand new, expensive Rojo seat cushion for my scooter. It had just come in the mail the day before. The nurse volunteered to clean it. I thought it was hopeless. I wasn't even sure I wanted it back! Fortunately we found out that it was made of a washable fabric cover over a rubber insert. Soon it was clean and much more comfortable than the original scooter seat.

We also found out that it is very important to check and recheck the valve on a catheter bag when it is emptied or changed. Otherwise you might also be saying, *"Noah, where's your ark?"*

Adapted Fitness Center

A year ago I learned about the Adapted Fitness Center at a local community college. This is a small room next to the school's regular student fitness center. All the equipment is specially designed to "adapt" to those people with special needs, particularly those in wheelchairs.

Some clever person in the marketing department must have come up with the name "adapted" instead of just the standard "handicapped" wording. I'm glad they came up with the name because when I'm there, I get a solid workout, so I don't feel handicapped – just tired!

Two wonderful people run the center on alternating days. The first step is to register for a special one credit hour class at the college. Then the main instructor does an evaluation with you in the fitness center. You tell her your background and explain any special needs. Then she designs an exercise program just for you, writing it down on a large card. She shows you how each machine works, explains your settings and lets you try it out. Each time you come into the center you sign in with your

ID card, get your exercise card from the file, and go through the program.

Along with the main instructor, there are several student helpers that find your card, put it on a clipboard and come over whenever you change machines to set the weight and do whatever is needed to get you started. The helpers wander around making sure everyone's doing OK, making adjustments as needed.

The "adaptive" technology of these machines is very simple, but very clever. All the seats are designed to swing well out of the way to allow a wheelchair to pull up. I've used both my scooter and power chair. The chair fits better with the machines. I can concentrate on doing the exercise, forgetting for the moment that I'm even in a wheelchair.

The best thing about the center is the atmosphere and the attitude of the staff and students. No one is treated like they are "handicapped." The atmosphere is positive, friendly and supportive. The first time I came, I was introduced to everyone. Instead of being competitive, everyone cheers for everyone else. If you accomplish any little thing, you get a certificate. I received one for going up on the weights for a specific machine. They even had an Olympics competition during the regular Olympics. I competed against my own record on the lat pull machine and received my medal at an Olympics luncheon – talk about making you feel special!

All the hugs and smiles were amazing. I felt like part of a family. All the encouragement makes me want to come back each time. I miss the people as well as the workout if I can't go. Sometimes I feel wimpy, and dread going. But once I'm there I'm glad I came, and I always feel better afterwards.

At first it was confusing, but at each machine someone was there to set it up, answer any questions, and give me an encouraging smile.

No, this is not your "normal" gym – *it's so much better!*

Trip to the Store

When I got a new set of wheels (no, not a tricked out Mustang or a fancy Corvette – we're talking about a large, bulky power wheelchair), the idea was that I would be able to go to either the corner drugstore in one direction or the shopping mall in the other direction from my house. The drugstore was only about six blocks away down mostly side streets.

The last two blocks were on a main street, but there were good sidewalks and a light to cross at the corner. There were several other stores at the corner as well – two fast-food drive-ins (roll-ins?), a video store, and two other really useful stores for me- a gas station and my favorite, a bowling alley!

In the other direction was a large shopping center, with a Target, movie theaters, several restaurants, my vitamin store, many smaller stores, and a pet store (no pets in our house right now, but since I could now get to the store...). This location was less than a mile away, down a two-lane street with good sidewalks and across several big parking lots.

The intent was that the trips would be easy for me to do on my own, thus giving me back a little of my former independence. Well, we all know how "easy" things are when you travel by wheelchair, no matter how big and fancy it is.

I talked with my wonderful friend Kay about making the trip. I was hesitant to do it by myself, at least the first time. The next time she came by for a visit, she showed up wearing her tennis shoes and track suit, ready for a trip to the corner drug store. We planned to stop for lunch at the Sonic drive-in next to the drug store, and sit at a picnic table to enjoy the cuisine (chili dogs, etc.). One advantage of living in Phoenix is predictable sunny weather for sitting outside.

Our first clue of how this MSAdventure would work out came right away – the city had picked this day to tar the cracks in our neighborhood streets! So when Kay tried to get to my house, she had to dodge the awful-smelling tar trucks and avoid the workmen blocking my street. It took a while before she could even get into my driveway.

It was a beautiful sunny day in November when we started our little trek. As we walked and rolled out my front door, I saw the next obstacle – it was garbage day. Everyone had rolled their big green garbage cans down the driveway to the curb, totally blocking the sidewalk.

Now for most people it isn't an issue to simply walk around the trash cans. They can step off the curb to the street or onto the grass or rocks on the other side. I don't have this flexibility.

From my front door we turned right to go around the block to avoid the tar trucks. Sounds simple, right? We immediately encountered our first trash can, so Kay went in front of me to move the big trash can out of the way. Kay is thin and petite with pretty short white hair. She looked like David battling Goliath moving those big green trash cans around!

As we turned the corner, Kay made a comment about how she understood now why I have problems getting around. She had no idea what she was in for! As she moved the third can, we saw an immovable object – a pickup truck with a trailer in the next driveway just blocking the sidewalk. However Kay is an irresistible force. She saw the man who lives there and asked him to pull the truck up so I could get by, which of course he did – who could turn down sweet Kay?

After seeing more obstacles ahead, we decided it would be better to go down the street. Let's talk curbs. Going down the slanted curb in my wheelchair is a challenge. It's scary for me, because it feels like I'm either going to do a somersault out of the chair or the chair is going to roll over with me in it. If I don't get it perfectly straight, the chair could tip over at an angle. So I need to have someone walking next to me ready to hang onto the chair in case it tips. So much for independence!

So with Kay beside me, I braved the steep curb. Amazing all the bumps, holes, rocks, trash and cracks (hence the tar trucks) that you find in the street when you are not driving. Kay and I found everything except the new earring I had lost a week ago when my husband and I were out for a walk and roll!

As I mentioned, Phoenix is normally warm (usually far more than warm) especially on a nice sunny day, so Kay and I were just wearing light sweaters. But as we turned the corner onto the main street we were hit by a blast of icy, cold air. After putting up with the chilly headwind (is this Arizona or Alaska?) and narrow sidewalk with sharp drop-offs at the edge, we finally we reached the corner drug store.

After our shopping we had planned on having a nice leisurely lunch at the Sonic picnic tables, but this idea was quickly vetoed due to chilled bodies. Instead we courageously crossed the street again so we could eat INSIDE at McDonald's. I admit it – we are officially desert wimps.

In an attempt to avoid the strong wind, we went home down the other busy street, thus making a big loop. It was a relief to turn down a smaller street so we could go side-by-side and actually talk to each other while avoiding cracks, holes, etc. We finally reached my block. End of adventure? Not quite. I couldn't stay in the street where the tar was fresh, so at the corner we used the ramp to the sidewalk. The city had recently installed ramps at some of the corners so I didn't have to ascend the treacherous curb.

After moving aside more trash cans and a "portable" basketball hoop, we made it home at last. With a big sigh of relief, Kay said I should write a book about my adventures. I promised if I ever did, she and our little adventure would be in it. *Kay, this one's for you! Thanks for your unflinching friendship and for battling the trash cans for me.*

Wide Load Ahead

Big Wheels

I never thought of myself as a collector of vehicles. Isn't that title reserved for rich stars like Jay Leno? However, my collection has been steadily growing.

My first mobility aid was a cane. I never pictured myself using a cane, much less at 42 years old. But the weakness in my left side and worsening problems with my left knee, and subsequently my balance, made the cane necessary. I refused to get one of those ugly, grey hospital canes. Not my color scheme at all – I'm a "Spring", light pastels, golden tones. I managed to find a nice copper-toned cane at a local drugstore. That wasn't quite as embarrassing to carry around. A while later my physical therapist got scratched off my list of favorite people when she insisted that I switch to a walker – now I really felt 92 instead of 42! Again, I refused to get a dull, hospital grey walker – or any walker. Then my good buddy LuAnn calmly took me to another drugstore that had a large selection of all types of mobility aids, including several different walkers. We managed to find a pretty blue one, which soon became my new best friend – and my first set of special wheels. LuAnn, with her special knack of making everything more fun, named her the "Blue Bomber." I grudgingly have to admit my back felt better than when I used the cane, and the seat became more and more welcome.

Then came the "Humpty Dumpty" incident (see prior chapter with that name). After that my fear of falling backwards made a walker not sufficient any more. A TV commercial convinced me to order a small three-wheeled scooter. I could get it in any color, as long as I wanted red! "Big Red" soon came in the mail. Of course LuAnn had to test her out in the parking lot (after all, she had taken a course at the Bob Bondurant School of High Performance Driving, so she was a driving expert).

My Blue Bomber never did fit through my bathroom doorway, but with some fancy maneuvering, Big Red could successfully get me to that critical place. I was still working at the time, so Big Red even went to work with me. However, since the warranty on most scooters is only one year, some major problem always seemed to develop at that time. I am now on my 4th scooter! (Big Red, Big Red II, the Silver Flash, and Baby Blue)

Again on TV I saw commercials for a power wheelchair. Grey Fox became my next set of wheels. It was more comfortable and could go further than the little scooter. But the drawback was that it was much bigger, so it wouldn't go into my bathroom. We requested a fancy option for an "elevator" which raised the chair about 6 inches. I pictured this being quite useful in the kitchen to help me reach things. However the first time I tried to use it in the kitchen, the footplate, which stuck out in the front, hit the bottom section of the stove, and broke it in two. Sigh. My husband glued the piece back together, but I'm afraid to take the Grey Fox into the kitchen any more. I only use it when I'm going out.

Now I had indoor wheels and outdoor wheels. Unfortunately the stiffness in my legs made it quite difficult for me to switch back and forth by myself, so I just stayed in Baby Blue, the scooter, most of the day.

When I developed edema (swelling) in my feet, I needed to find a way to elevate them during the day. I wasn't able to get them on a stool or the couch by myself, so my doctor recommended some new wheels to add to my collection. This was a power wheelchair with a special feature that would raise my legs in an attempt to defeat the effects of gravity.

When the salesman brought one to my home to try, I was shocked to see it – it looked like a big, black spider monster! It was huge with many arms and other attachments ready to grab me and not let go. My claustrophobia kicked in to start a panic attack. Now I'm not usually such a drama queen, but this device was overwhelming.

The salesman calmly explained that the chair came this way, but I wouldn't need all the attachments. I could also get narrower arm pads. It has taken several tries, and it still doesn't fit me quite right, or go into my bathroom, but this new chair does raise my legs. And I was able to order it in purple (a small section of metal frame), so it's not all scary black. We call her Violet.

We've also had to buy a beautiful blue minivan to transport all the big wheels. Ariel is equipped with a fold-out ramp on the side. Finding the correct type of parking space to accommodate this is another story. I would so like to drive this new vehicle, but I'm afraid Ariel is destined to be my chauffer-driven limousine. I try very hard not to be a backseat driver from the passenger side, but it's difficult when it's my car. How lucky I am to have friends willing to give up their time and put up with helping me in and out of my wheelchair and van in order to get me to all my doctor appointments.

My house now looks like a wheelchair store display. One is rear-wheel drive, another front-wheel drive and the third center-wheel drive. This gives me my daily driving challenge. Each of my big wheels does some functions very well and others not. So depending on my needs at the time, and if a lovely assistant is available to help me transfer, I certainly have a selection from which to choose. Let's see, which big wheel matches my outfit today – *the grey, the blue or the more formal basic black (with a touch of purple)?*

Invisible

It's amazing that for such a wide load, my big wheelchair and I can sometimes turn invisible!

When does this happen? Sometimes it's in the grocery store. As part of Murphy's Law for MS, whenever I need to reach for something from a shelf, the specific item I need is always on the top shelf. Of all the various items in the store, how could this work out that way?

What am I to do? I can't stand up any more, so that's out. My handy little grabber tool is at home, so that doesn't help. I don't really trust it for grabbing things off of a shelf anyway. I'm afraid I would either end up with flat bread instead of normal fluffy bread, or I would be hearing, "Clean up on aisle 12 – spaghetti sauce broken and spilled on floor and all over customer in wheelchair – bring mop and towel!"

Usually there are a lot of other people around trying to push their big carts past the wheelchair which always seems to be in the way or stuck behind a display of breakable objects. Once people get over the shock of someone in the wheelchair talking to them, they're usually very helpful about reaching something for me. But, once again, whenever I need assistance, all the people blocking my path have suddenly melted into the background. Everywhere I look no one is nearby. An amazing disappearing act any magician would be proud of!

Another time this happens is when I need to go through a doorway. Most places don't have those wonderful little handicapped buttons that will magically open the doors when pushed. Even if they do, sometimes the door still doesn't open. So I'm left struggling to try to open the door myself and get all the way through it before it closes on me. If that doesn't work, then I'm left sitting around waiting for someone to either come in or go out so I can follow them.

Now to be fair, some people go out of their way to help me, even without being asked. When I went to the doctor's office last week I had a MSAdventure trying to get into the office.

My wonderful friend, Lorette, had dropped me off out in front of the 26-story office building. Their parking garage is horrible, so she usually drops me off in the driveway and goes down the street to hang out at McDonald's reading her newspaper while I'm in the doctor's office. Then I call her when I'm done so she can pick me up out front.

This usually is no problem for me since this building is one with those handy little buttons to open the big glass doors. However this particular day the window washers had set up their equipment to wash all the windows. They were currently washing one side of the triangle tower, but had evidently just finished washing above the doorways. There was yellow tape saying, "Do not cross" all the way across the doorways.

Imagine my surprise when I came up the long ramp from the driveway to confront yellow tape. The usually crowded doorways were eerily quiet. I wondered how I would get inside for my appointment.

Just then a nice young man came walking over to me. He said there was another doorway to enter the building and that he would show me. We had only gone a few feet when he stopped and asked me to wait while he checked something. I watched while he walked ahead looking around. To my chagrin, what I saw straight ahead was a set of about six steps leading down to a courtyard, then back up to get to the other doorway.

My would-be hero came back to tell me he tried to find a ramp, but there wasn't one that would allow us to get to the other doorway. So he did the next best thing – he held up the yellow tape so I could get under it, then opened the door for me. On the way out, after my appointment, the building was busy with the lunchtime crowds. The yellow tape was still up, but I was once again invisible. So I went back into the lobby to ask a security guard to hold up the tape so I could get back out to the waiting car.

I'm forever thankful to the heroes that see through my "invisibility" to appear out of nowhere when I get *trapped in a MSAdvemture.*

Weighing In

Do you remember those trips to the doctor's office? The first thing the nurse does as she's taking you to the examining room is to make a stop at – yes, the dreaded scale to get your weight.

Fighting the battle of the bulge most of my adult life, this was one step I never looked forward to. No matter how hard I tried to keep the weight off, the scale always seemed to hold bad news for me.

Once I could no longer stand on my own two feet, I gratefully had a solid excuse to skip this step. However when my neurologist recommended a new medication administered through an IV, she needed to know my exact weight to determine the correct dosage.

So now what was I to do? At their office, they had a big scale with a ramp that you could drive onto. Of course my little red scooter was just a bit too long to fit all the way onto the scale.

Hmm. What to do now?

They found a regular chair that would fit on the scale, so first they weighed the chair. Now how to get me onto it? Of course there were no strong, body-builders around. Since my scooter couldn't get up the little ramp to even get me close to the chair, first two little nurses helped me slide over from my scooter to a small rolling office chair.

Next they rolled me up the ramp, close to the chair. Now, I'm not all that overweight, but it was an awkward situation to get me from the rolling chair on the slanted ramp onto the weigh-in chair. It took three little nurses to accomplish the move. It must have been quite the sight! Finally they could operate the scale. Thankfully they remembered to subtract the weight of the chair before writing the number down in my chart.

Now, the whole process had to be reversed!

Could there possibly be other, hopefully easier, methods to weigh someone in a wheelchair?

When I was in the rehab hospital a while ago, they rolled me back and forth on the bed to get me into a sling. Then a machine with a hook lifted the sling. I felt like a new baby being delivered by the stork! But it's not worth going to rehab just to find out my weight.

A year ago when I was hospitalized with severe pneumonia, the beds were actually smart enough to get my weight without even moving me. How easy was that?

Again, it's definitely not worth being hospitalized just to get weighed!

I've recently managed to lose some weight. So for the first time I actually wanted to find out what I weighed – I was anticipating good news for once.

One of my doctors told me that the hospital had a special scale they could use to weigh my big black wheelchair that I was currently using. This way they could get the weight of my chair by itself, so the next time I needed to be weighed, all I would need to do was get weighed in my chair and subtract the difference.

Sounded like an easy solution. I had an upcoming appointment with my neurologist, whose office was right next to the hospital. I thought I would just stop by there on the way to my appointment.

To save time, I called the hospital first to find out exactly where the scale was located. The operator was perplexed about where to connect me, so I was put on hold for several minutes. Finally she said the only scale they had that was big enough to handle the wheelchair was located in the Receiving Department at the loading dock. The loading dock! Talk about a blow to my self-image!

When she connected me, the man was surprised at my unusual request, but remembered nurses bringing patients down there before. When I asked the doctor and nurse about it, they agreed to do it, but were short-staffed that day, so didn't have enough people to help get me in and out of my chair.

So for now I'll just have to keep guessing when asked my weight. The next time I see that doctor, I also have a *date with the loading dock!*

Feeling Rundown?

Not being able to drive my car any more was a giant blow to my sense of independence and self worth. I hated being dependent on someone else for transportation all the time. Therefore whenever I was out and about on my scooter or power chair, I tried to take advantage of the opportunity by combining stops at nearby stores.

There was usually a Walgreens drug store near any doctor's office. I've found almost everything I need at Walgreens, from toothpaste to greeting cards to Diet Coke and snacks. Oh - they also do my retail prescription drugs.

When I take a bus to my doctor's appointments, I'm usually left with extra time before the bus picks me up to take me home. This can be an excellent opportunity for a little Walgreens shopping. In order to get between the doctor's office and the store, there is typically a street to cross. Since any situation can turn into a MSAdventure, this is no exception.

One day I had plenty of time before my bus, and Valentine's Day was coming, so I decided to make the trek from the doctor's office to Walgreens for some cards, little gifts for my loved ones, and whatever treasures I could spot that day.

To do this, I had to cross at a small intersection – one small street and a larger street. I always crossed at a crosswalk with a walk signal to be safe – or so I thought. I waited for the walk signal and made sure no one was turning right on red before starting across the four lanes of traffic on my little scooter.

I was almost across the first two lanes to the center of the street when a car came speeding out from the small side street, making a left turn into the lane I was currently crossing. She was the stereotypical woman driver – talking to and looking at her passenger instead of the road in front of her. All I could do was stop and brace for impact while I stared at her in terror.

Amazing what you think of at a time like that. I'd been having a lot of trouble with my old scooter so we finally bought a new one. Now the thought went through my head, "Darn – now we're going to have to buy another new scooter!"

At the last second the woman looked up, saw me and hit the brakes, stopping with a couple of inches to spare. She motioned for me to go ahead to finish crossing the street, glaring at me for having the nerve to make her test her brakes. I hurried as quickly as my little scooter would carry me, trying to remember how to breathe again. It's a good thing I wasn't getting my blood pressure checked right then – the little blood pressure cuff wouldn't have survived!

A few weeks later I once again needed to cross the street to get from my massage therapy session to - you guessed it - Walgreens. This time it was a very large street, but had a good wide crosswalk with a lot of visibility. I made it safely across the first half of the street with plenty of time left on the walk signal.

As I started across the second half, I heard sirens getting louder and louder. I looked down the oncoming lanes I was crossing to see an ambulance and fire truck headed straight for me. There I was, out in the middle of the street. It was too late to turn back, and I didn't want to get flattened, so I raced as fast as I could to get across. I made it to the sidewalk and a fast food parking lot as the super loud sirens squealed by.

I crossed the restaurant parking lot to the Walgreens parking lot – then I saw where the fire department had been going – to the Walgreens! I had to work my way around the fire trucks to get into the store. Evidently one of the customers had been having medical problems. I'm glad the store wasn't on fire.

After my ten minutes of shopping, I went outside to look for the bus. I spotted it pulling into the far side of the parking lot. The driver was obviously trying to figure out how to come to pick me up with the fire trucks blocking the entrance. I tried to go out into the parking lot so he could pick me up, but either he didn't see me or thought I was just some crazy lunatic driving a scooter around the parking lot. The bus finally stopped behind the fire trucks. I carefully made my way around to it and finally headed for home.

As much as I enjoy my feeling of independence, *I'm re-thinking my little trips to Walgreens!*

Doorways (Caution: Wide Load Ahead)

Do you remember seeing those flashing lights on the freeway warning you that there was a vehicle on the road up ahead that didn't fit the lane in the usual way? That's how I feel frolicking around in my handy wheelchair.

Doorways. Never used to think about them. Now that one word can trigger concern, worry or downright panic. It's bad enough feeling that your body is a bit too wide, but when you put that body in a big bulky wheelchair, it brings new meaning to the words, "wide load."

Have you ever paid much attention to how wide a doorway is? I only did on moving day, trying to drag a queen-sized bed into a small apartment – up a narrow flight of stairs, of course! Now I have five different sets of wheels – two power chairs, one scooter, one manual wheelchair and a walker. Only the scooter will fit through the bathroom doorway – with difficulty!

For a couple of years I had heard about some special

hinges that would give more space to the doorway. It took a while for me to find these elusive pieces of hardware. Finally, I found them on the internet and picked them up at a local warehouse. Theoretically all that was needed to install the new hinges was to replace the ones currently in use on the door and the wall with the new ones, even using the same screws.

Well, we all know how little fix-it projects work out. First of all, the new hinges were a little different size, so my husband had to chisel out the indentation on the door to fit them. Then he had to find one more screw for each hinge. The end result, however, was very successful. With the new hinges, the door swung out of the way, leaving the doorway an inch or so wider and simpler to pass through. I still can only use my scooter for the bathroom. The doorway is now wide enough for a wheelchair to fit through, but the narrow hallway doesn't allow enough space to make the 90 degree turn. The new hinges make it easier for the scooter to pass through and save some gouges in the door and frame.

Let's talk thresholds. They add a whole new dimension to the doorway dilemma, bridging the gap between the room and the outside surface. With a threshold you might be going from room to room or even out of a building. Again, it's amazing the things you never used to notice – until you were forced to.

Thresholds can be made of wood or metal and are usually a raised surface of varying shapes and heights. Not a big deal when all you do is just step over them. However if your stepper is broken, this can be a challenge. The curved, smooth thresholds are the easiest to maneuver with a wheelchair. Others could have sharp edges or metal tracks which can catch the wheels or make for a bumpy ride. One technique for getting over the threshold that usually works quite well is to lay either a large piece of carpeting or a heavy doormat across the threshold and over the steps (I just happen to have one in my purse!).

Once over the threshold starts the real challenge. Outside is a brave new world with its own obstacles – are there steps? How many? How high is each step? Is there a ramp? If so, how steep is the ramp? Is it made of slippery material? Is it raining? My husband has become quite adept at building little ramps. We take one with us if we go to someone else's house. Note: sometimes a little creativity helps – an impromptu ramp can make good use of all those phone books that you never use! You can also use plywood or boards to bridge the steps if they are too tall or wide.

So make your way up the ramp, over the steps and through the doorway to *cross the threshold for an exciting MSadventure!*

Take a Seat

"Take a Seat." "No, thanks, I brought my own." That's the "Smart Alec" response that pops into my mind (but usually don't say) whenever someone says that to me. This phrase is one of the useless phrases when talking to someone in a wheelchair.

Just where are these "seats" we are being offered? They must be some place special for us special people. Just look for the lovely handicapped symbol. You never know where we'll be.

At the baseball game, you have two choices for the basic handicapped seating. One choice is on the same level as the entry from the street. This is very convenient. No elevators, easy access to bathrooms, food stands, and team shop (have to get that team jersey, etc.). Unfortunately when you get to the seating area to watch the game, it's in row 40.

But don't worry if you can't see the field clearly. Replays and other fun things will be displayed on the huge

Jumbotron display. The only problem with that is from the handicapped seating area, when you look up at the screen, all you can see is the balcony seating above you.

There is another interesting option: the handicapped seating area behind right field. This is on the ground floor – literally. From here you get a wonderful view of the right fielder's backside! If you're lucky, the ball will be hit to deep right field, so you can meet him personally as he backs up into the fence separating you. Definitely feels like you're part of the game here.

However, being on the ground level makes it difficult to see the rest of the field. Oh, but there are replays on the Jumbotron – sorry, it's directly to the side, so it's once again not visible from these seats. You are, however, right next to the swimming pool (yes, it's Phoenix, Arizona, so we have a swimming pool inside our baseball park). You won't be able to use it, but you will meet your neighbors in their swimsuits as they share your bathroom.

What about when you go to see a play or concert? This can also get quite interesting. My daughter's college graduation was held in Grady Gammage Auditorium, where they have plays and other performances at Arizona State University. This building was designed by the famous Frank Lloyd Wright. With all the awards it received, you'd think it must have been designed wonderfully. Let's see.

To get to the handicapped seating area, we followed the signs in the lobby to a back corner where we were escorted down a narrow hallway to a very tiny elevator – just barely enough room for my wheelchair and two other people. My claustrophobia kicked in big time. Finally the doors opened to another narrow hallway leading to the main auditorium. The handicapped seating area was directly in front of the first row of seats.

We thought we would get a great view of the stage. However, the stage was about five feet high, with the foot lights another six inches higher, extending all the way across the stage. I gave the camera to my husband, who was sitting back several rows, so on the camera, the people on the stage would have feet! After looking up at the stage all evening, a good neck massage would have felt great. I guarantee the esteemed Mr. Wright never watched a performance in his theater from a wheelchair!

Handicapped seating will always be a mystery to solve. Often it will be at the very front or the very back. At my daughter's dance recital, with the seating directly in front of the stage, I could see everything but her feet!

However, every now and then you'll get a great view from the handicapped area, and all the people in the regular seats will be handing you their cameras. So no matter where you get seated, just be thankful there is a way for you to get into the building, and *enjoy the show!*

Tough Act to Swallow

Have you ever wondered what happens when you swallow? If so, you need to get a life! I had the rare opportunity to see what actually goes on behind the scenes in my throat when I swallow.

When I was admitted to the hospital recently with pneumonia, they wanted to make sure that I didn't cause it myself by aspirating my food – breathing it down my airway into my lungs instead of swallowing it down my esophagus to my stomach.

First we took a long gurney ride through the mysterious back hallways of the hospital, in and out of the elevator, and then left in a tiny back room. The gurney rides were always an experience. The hallways seemed endless and confusing. The gurney was quite a challenge to get in and out of the elevator, around corners, past obstacles (like other gurneys). The people we passed stared, wondering what awful illness I had or what injury happened to me, while I thought the same about them. Finally I was left in a tiny back room wondering if this rat would ever find her way out of the maze back to her room to see daylight again.

Eventually they came back for me and transferred me to a wheelchair, because the next room they took me to was even smaller! It was full of equipment and machines. Four or five people were there – all to watch me swallow! Gulp. They gave me little mouthfuls of liquids of various consistencies, adding thickeners as needed. I was in front of some type of x-ray machine which displayed the inner workings of my throat while I swallowed. At first I couldn't see the monitor – just heard them all talking about what they saw. I finally asked if I could see, too. They seemed surprised that I wanted to see – it is my body, after all. So they turned a monitor so I could see as well, and answered any questions I had. Until then I just felt like someone's science experiment.

I thought when I swallowed, the food simply went down my esophagus to my stomach and that was it. However it appears to be more complicated than that. They told me that my tongue can move in different ways when I swallow, either helping or hindering the process. There is a little pocket in my throat where food residue can get caught. Sometimes I had to swallow several times or take a sip of water to get the food on its way to my stomach.

It was strange, but interesting in a weird sort of way to watch all this happening inside of my throat on the TV monitor. It was even more wild than some of the strange channels on cable TV! The conclusion by this team of highly qualified swallowing experts was that my swallowing equipment appeared to be functioning correctly.

Just to make sure, they had me sit in a special section of the cafeteria at lunchtime for the next several days. This section was reserved for those patients who might need help or have problems eating (or swallowing). Several helpers, including respiratory specialists, were on hand to help or observe. I've never liked being the center of attention. Knowing that someone was there watching me swallow made me very aware of each bite I swallowed, at least at first.

One advantage of being in this "select group" of patients is that we didn't have to wait in the normal long cafeteria line. If I got there right away, I could pass by everyone else in line and be first in the food line. This did not help me make friends with all the hungry, bored people waiting in line. Since I did not start out as a regular member of this group, I was the recipient of many glares and had to apologize and explain myself as I went to the front. Often a staff member would tell me to get back in line until I went through my explanation.

I was relieved when they decided that I wasn't going to breathe in my lunch, and I could sit at the regular tables again. It's better for my swallowing and digestion to put up with cold food rather than cold, angry stares from hungry people! I'm very aware of my swallowing now. *I sure don't take swallowing for granted any more.*

So What's Bugging You?

So what's bugging you? One problem living in the desert is that we occasionally have big black beetles that decide it's much more fun exploring a nice cool house than staying outside with the cactus. I've been getting attacked by some for the last week. My brave husband, Steve, just made minced meat out of two of them, but there's now another one that comes after me in the kitchen when I least expect it. I've dreaded going in there at night or early in the morning. Since I'm never up in the night or early morning that shouldn't be an issue, right? Yeah, right. Earlier (it's only 5am now) the nasty critter came after me in the kitchen again. I'm not coordinated or mobile enough to get it with the fly swatter any more.

I came out to the living room about 15 minutes ago to write an email on my laptop. I didn't bring any food with me, so I was quite surprised when I saw the annoying bug coming up to me again! It knew I couldn't get it, so it was enjoying terrorizing me. I went out to the kitchen to get the fly swatter. By the time I got back, the bug was moseying back towards the kitchen (it missed me). I was able to get close enough to get a few good whacks in. It looked like I was successful, so I went back to my computer. Then the nasty critter got up and started moving again. (If cats have nine lives, how many do bugs have?)

Of course when I had tried to set the fly swatter down earlier, I dropped it on the floor near the bug. So now I had to try to pick it up off the floor (never a simple task for me in my scooter) while the bug was making its getaway. I finally managed to pick up the fly swatter and get in some more good whacks. It hasn't moved for a while, so I think I was finally successful. I'll have to wait for my husband to get up to remove the remains.

So is your morning as exciting as mine? I've been up since about 3am. Later this morning a friend will be over to help me take a shower. What a thrilling life I lead!

Oh, good grief! Mr. Nasty just started moving again. At least the fly swatter hadn't fallen all the way to the floor yet, so I squashed the bug some more. It will be another 25 minutes before Steve gets up to get rid of it. Sigh.

Did you enjoy hearing about my bug trauma? I didn't intend on bugging my book, but I guess this would qualify as a MSAdventure. After all, the bug was taking advantage of my limited mobility to taunt me. I could hear it going, *"Nanny, nanny, nanny – you can't get me!"* *while it ran under my scooter.*

The Adventures Continue

Fun on the Bus

Most people have seen the special busses that stop for disabled (awful label, isn't it?) people. You know the ones – always blocking your way in parking lots or in front of doctor's offices or blocking your vision on the roads. Who are those special people that get this fancy door-to-door service anyway? Well, I hereby apologize for all the inconvenience – it's just me.

For those who do not understand this service, let me try to explain. There are several bus services that will pick up handicapped (another awful label) people from their homes (or anywhere) and drop them off where they need to go, such as doctor's appointments, the store, etc. - even the racetrack (that passenger claimed he worked there – yeah, right!). Then the busses will return to pick them up again later (sometimes questionable).

The first step is to make a reservation. No that's not right, before that you need to get all your paperwork completed so that you will be allowed to make a reservation. It's been a while, so I forgot that interesting step. First I had to get a letter from my doctor stating that I was disabled (just sitting in a wheelchair isn't good enough – anyone could do that). This letter had to be brought in person to a bus office so that I could get a disabled bus pass ID card. The closest office for me was at an obscure shopping center about an hour away. Instead of low to high, the speed control on my wheelchair goes from turtle to bunny. But even on "bunny", it's not quite fast enough for the freeway!

So how was I to get there without a bus pass? Well, the bus company generously offered a free ride to their office for this purpose. So one day I made this journey and got my special bus ID card. I was told to carry this with me every time I ride the bus. I don't think anyone has ever asked to see it. They also gave me an ID number with an expiration date.

Back to making a reservation. First you have to know the rules –and follow them. Every bus system is different, so beware. For mine, you can only make a reservation up to 2 weeks ahead, from 8am – 6pm, Monday – Friday. And you'd better be on the phone at 8am. When you call you must give them your name, bus ID #, expiration date, and finally where you're going and the time of your appointment (if you're seeing a doctor). Then they will tell you what time is available for pickup.

It was quite a shock to me at first how far in advance they wanted to pick me up. Part of the reason is that you never know how long the trip will take, due to traffic, weather, or other passengers to be dropped off, picked up, not ready, etc. To be fair, they want you to get to your appointment on time. The return trip is similar – you never know how long the appointment will take, so you need to allow extra time to be sure you're ready to leave when the bus comes for you. The bottom line is - get used to it and deal with it! I've devoted an entire chapter (see "Waiting") on things to do while waiting for the bus.

So now you've got a reservation. Be ready before the pickup time. If you're ready, the bus will be late. If you're not quite ready for whatever reason (something unexpected always happens at the last moment), the bus will come early (see chapter "Murphy's Law for MS").

When the bus comes, the next challenge is getting on it. If you're mobile, just walk up the steps and sit down like regular people do. If you're in a wheelchair, it's a bit more complicated. The bus comes with a very handy platform which folds out of the side and lowers down to the ground. Since the bus is narrow inside, I back my little scooter onto the platform, and then back into the bus. This can get tricky if there are already other passengers or wheelchairs on the bus. Ignore them and any comments.

Inside the bus, there are regular seats in the back half. The front half has space behind the driver's seat for wheelchairs. When I first started taking the bus, the drivers asked me to sit in the regular seats. So I would back my scooter down the aisle and transfer sideways to a seat. This wasn't easy, but I was able to do it. However getting back onto my scooter to get off the bus was a different matter. The scooter seat was a little higher than the bus seat. This made it very difficult for me to do the transfer. Finally I had to tell them I wasn't able to transfer. This got me a lecture each time I boarded a bus on how it wasn't safe to stay in my scooter, so I would be traveling at my own risk. Then they would finally use the tie-down straps – all four of them, and the seat belt and a shoulder harness.

Now – we are ALMOST ready for our journey. Before you can begin the trip you need to pay the driver – exact change only, please. Then verify your destination. Now, off to see how many stops and/or passengers we can pick up before getting to our stop. Sometimes the other passengers can be friendly, helpful or entertaining. Other times just the opposite. Either way, be glad you're on your way.

The best part of the trip is when you pull up in front of your own house. The drivers will walk you to the door, carry your bags if any, or even push your chair (see chapter "An Aisle Too Far"). Be glad you're home and glad there is a bus system and drivers that will get you safely to and from. *And just think of all the MSAdventures you can have while you're out!*

Waiting

Typically, there will be waiting time when you take the handicapped bus anywhere. So come prepared with things to do or the time will seem endless.

First you will need something to do while you are nervously waiting for the bus to show up at your house – assuming you are ready on time (which will cause the bus to be late). Make it something you can put away quickly as soon as the bus pulls up, such as the newspaper or a magazine. This will keep your starting stress level lower. Now would not be the time for a complicated knitting project.

In the bus, some lucky people are able to read to pass the time – I'm not one of them. The noise level in the bus will not be conducive to conversation, especially with the bus driver (don't annoy the drivers – they are busy working for you). If you are an outgoing, friendly person (not me), other passengers might help you pass the time. But they can also be quite annoying – which also passes the time, only more slowly!

Try mentally planning the rest of your day, or pretend you are the tour guide describing your trip.

While waiting at the doctor's office, you'll need something to occupy yourself, other than worrying about the bad test results the doctor is about to give you. I find a good trashy, lightweight paperback works well. It will keep your attention away from the annoying people around you and what kind of germs they are coughing on you today. The book can be quickly tucked away when your name is called.

Sometimes you get lucky and interesting things find you. When I arrived at the doctor's office way early one time I was surprised to see two long tables set up behind the security guard, in front of the elevators. There was a girl setting up displays of jewelry she had designed. I had fun using my waiting time shopping – five pairs of earrings and two beautiful necklaces later, the bus came.

One day while waiting for the bus to pick me up from church, I thought I would put the time to good use. We had started a new Bible study class that day, which meant that I had a new book to read and homework to do. I found what I thought was the perfect place to study. It was almost noon, but I found a spot in the shade (essential in Phoenix) alongside the church on a big sidewalk between two large grassy areas. I had a good view of where the bus would come in to pick me up.

The birds were singing, flowers were blooming, a gentle breeze was blowing. Ideal situation, right? I opened my brand new book and propped the workbook on my lap. All of a sudden I heard a strange noise. It was a sunny day, but I was soon caught in a rainstorm – the sprinklers on both sides of me had come on! So much for my brand new book, workbook, and lovely hair style! I frantically gathered up my things, powered up my scooter and headed for cover. Needless to say, it was a long, soggy trip home that day!

Finally the last step of any journey is the wait for the ride home. This is usually done outside, watching anxiously for the bus. You need to be alert, because sometimes the bus driver doesn't know exactly where you will be waiting, and you sure don't want him to drive by. I find this is an excellent time to count your blessings.

Find all the things to be thankful for on that day and in your life. Sometimes the day's been rough and you're tired now and probably hungry and/or thirsty, but try – it will end the day better. You made it to the doctor. The bus is on its way to take you home (believe this, or the wait seems longer). The weather could be worse. No one spilled their drink on you in the waiting room (unless someone did). Challenge yourself to think of as many positive thoughts as you can. Soon the bus will pull up and you will be headed home. That's the final blessing. *Hope you enjoyed the trip!*

It Takes a Village

When I first starting reading about how to deal with having MS, and in lectures I attended, they made a big deal out of encouraging you to have a support system. I felt like I needed a big crane to hold me up or a network of steel girders like some high rise skyscraper. It turns out that wasn't far from the truth. Just as they say, "It takes a village to raise a child", it also takes a village (or a small army) to support a person with MS.

One level of support is the team of doctors and other health care professionals that you develop. (see prior chapter "Team Sport") This is an ongoing ever-changing list. It's like jell-o – there's always room for more doctors on the list. Just not enough money to pay them all! As your needs change, you'll find different ones to provide whatever type of support you are lacking.

Another level of support will be your friends. I am so fortunate in the group of friends in my life. Some I've known before MS, such as my high school buddy, Jan. We haven't even lived in the same state since high school, but have kept in touch. When I talk with her, I feel like my old self, and don't think about having MS. What a nice vacation from those thoughts.

Other friends I used to do things with that I can't do any more. Sadly some of them you lose touch with when you no longer have that activity in common. Others you will find things holding your friendship together besides that original link. Helen is my sailing buddy. In my previous life before MS, I was a Red Cross certified sailing instructor and taught sailing at summer camps. Although Helen and I don't go sailing together any more, we will always be close friends.

My church friends are one of my strongest levels of support. Whatever your beliefs, your spiritual life is nothing that can be touched by MS. In fact mine has definitely gotten stronger. I don't need my wheelchair in this part of my life. These friends support me emotionally and spiritually, and also very practically by giving me a ride to the doctor or the gym or the store, or even by rubbing my poor swollen feet!

New people will also come into your life just because you have MS. In this case, MS is the link holding this group to your support structure. Some are professionals that fit into that level. Others are people who share your MS situation. When I attend the Adapted Fitness

Center, I meet people who have special needs. There I've discovered that MS isn't the only disease that can be an adventure!

Finally my basic level of support, my foundation, is my family. My wonderful daughter, Laura, is the fun part of my life. When I first learned I had MS, it was a shock, of course, but she has always done whatever she could to help. As soon as she got her driver's license, she had to start driving me around. When she started pursuing her career as a broadcaster, she wanted to become famous so she could be a spokesperson for MS and raise money for research.

MS can challenge any marriage. It hasn't been easy, but my husband, Steve, remains firmly in my foundation. He has learned how to build ramps, maintain my vast array of motorized scooters and chairs, and adjust our lives as needed. He is my rock and my love.

You are the foreman of this massive project. It's up to you to take care of the infrastructure first. Get plenty of rest and eat the best things to keep your body healthy (dark chocolate and ice cream work wonders – for medicinal purposes only, of course). Consistently take the medications that you and your doctors have decided upon.

Do whatever it takes to keep each level of your support structure strong. When you find a new area of concern, either modify a current level to deal with it or add a new level of support. This is an ongoing, ever-changing project, so accept that and be willing to change and modify your life and your village as you need to. Don't get bogged down in resentment or self-pity – that will eat away and corrode your support beams. Instead enjoy those who are a part of your life, however they got there. *With an entire village, there is always someone there for you if you are willing to look.*

Nightmares

Recently I spent two long weeks in the hospital trying to recover from pneumonia. Despite all the efforts of the doctors and all the high-powered medicine being pumped into my system, I seemed to be getting worse.

Even though my body desperately needed sleep, my mind wouldn't settle down. During one of the worst nights, I woke from a horrible nightmare. The room was dark; only a small light shining in the hallway. I couldn't figure out where I was, but I knew this wasn't my bedroom at home.

Then someone walked by the doorway. It took a few seconds for me to recognize him as one of the nurses in the hospital. He had been one of my nurses for the past couple of days. Now the memories came flooding back along with overwhelming fears from the all-too-real nightmare.

I didn't want to be there in the dark room all alone.

Even though I was very tired, and knew I should get more sleep, I was afraid if I fell back asleep the awful nightmare would return. As the nurse walked by, he stopped in my room to check on me. I asked if he had a minute to stay and talk. He listened to my nightmare story and other fears. His calm reassuring voice eased my fears. For the rest of the long, dark night, he kept checking on me.

When I woke up the next morning (guess I finally fell asleep), I felt different. Then I remembered the long, difficult night. I looked for the nurse to thank him, but there had already been a shift change, so new nurses were on duty now.

So why did I feel differently? Then I knew - I wasn't as sick as I was before! For the first time I knew that I was going to get well. That horrible nightmare wasn't going to come true after all.

From that point on my health continued to improve. After a couple more days in the hospital, I was taken to a nearby rehab facility to continue healing. It took several weeks for the pneumonia to totally clear up and even longer for my energy level to return, but I was confident that I would heal up.

I never saw that nurse again. I hope he knows how much he helped me get through a dark scary night. Oh, did I tell you what his name was? *His name tag said, "Angel."*

Identity Theft

Have you seen the commercials on TV where a man gives you his social security number to prove that even if he tells you, you still won't be able to "steal" his identity to get credit cards or loans? Just call the 800 number on the screen to sign up for identity theft protection, pay the monthly fee and your worries are over.

Unfortunately life isn't quite that easy. Credit card thieves aren't the only ones that can steal your identity. Accidents or illnesses, such as MS, can also change your life so much that you lose yourself. Who is this person in the wheelchair? What happened to the person who used to teach sailing and play the guitar and sing and laugh?

Sometimes I look in a mirror and wonder who that person is. I feel lost. What happened to those dreams of traveling and hiking and playing with my grandchildren? When you lose your way, sometimes you need a little help to get back. My counselor tries to help me think of how to do some of the things I used to enjoy, like go to a baseball game. If you look, many venues have handicapped seating and they try to make things convenient.

Some things aren't as easy as they used to be, but that doesn't mean they are impossible. With a little extra planning, you can still enjoy those activities. I find myself worrying about the "what ifs" that could go wrong. Well, things can go wrong for anyone. You don't have a lock on having unexpected problems, just because you're not "normal."

Well, guess what – it is normal to have problems. Anyone could run out of gas or get lost or lose their tickets or not make it to the bathroom in time. Do what you can to avoid the problems you anticipate could happen. My counselor has taught me to pack a bag of essentials, including extra shorts, allergy pills, Tylenol, etc. Hopefully I'll never need my emergency supplies. I get tired of lugging the bag around everywhere, but it does ease my stress level to know I'm prepared for the problems I can anticipate. If others happen, I'll have to deal with it – just like everybody else does.

Attitude is crucial. If you think some activity is too much effort and it won't be much fun any more, then you're right – it won't be. Instead if you approach the situation with a sense of adventure, life can still be enjoyable and fun.

Bottom line – yes, there are things you won't be able to do any more and dreams that will have to stay dreams. Life is like that for everyone. Do some research. Find a way to still do some things you didn't think would work any more. Find new activities that will be easier to do. Don't give up on life just because it has changed. Use your imagination and the abilities you still possess to have some fun. How about this: make a difference in someone else's life! No matter your situation, you can still be a friend – no special abilities – or mobilities required. Everyone has problems and needs a friend.

So pack your bag of essentials – *don't forget your sense of humor wherever you packed it away, and go have a MSAdventure!*

To Sleep, Perchance to Dream

Question: In the daytime, if you dream about sleeping at night, is that still a "daydream"? Do I sound confused? That happens when you're suffering from sleep deprivation.

Recently I have had a lot of trouble getting a good night's sleep. I fall asleep, but then I wake up at 2 or 3 a.m. and end up staying up the rest of the day. I usually need to use the bathroom when I wake up. Just getting out of bed or my recliner is an ordeal. Then using the bathroom is never a simple task any more. So by the time I'm done, I'm pretty much awake. I know later in the day I will be a zombie, but right then I'm wide awake.

Other things that wake me up are muscle spasms and stiffness. Once I'm tucked in bed, my body doesn't move. This leads to very stiff muscles and other aches and pains. I even developed a pressure sore on my ankle bone from sleeping on my side. We have one of those air beds that's supposed to cure all discomforts. It used to work quite well in that department, but I guess my discomforts have won over the therapeutic abilities of the bed!

Well, when do I get any sleep? I seem to have perfected the art of falling asleep while sitting straight up in my scooter without falling off – at least not yet.

Yesterday I went to a new Bible study class with the women at my church. Class started with a video presentation. They turned off the lights and started the video. Then the lights came right back on again. My friend next to me asked what I thought of it. Thought of what? Evidently I had just slept right through the 30-minute presentation! Then I spent an hour with three women I'd never met before, discussing a topic I had just slept through. That's me – always making a good first impression!

I've found myself having other short lapses during the day. I'll realize I don't know what's gone on for the last five minutes or how the TV show I was watching ended and a new one started. Then there's my frequent brain fog when my brain just won't quite kick into gear. That's when I long to take a quick walk around the block to wake up. Riding around in my wheelchair just doesn't quite have the same effect.

So what do you do at 3 a.m. when you're supposed to be sleeping? I can't watch TV or do anything that makes noise or I'll wake up my husband who has to go to work in the morning. My eyes won't focus yet, so reading is out. Hey, how about writing a book? If nothing in this book makes much sense, I'm blaming it on the fact that most of it was written around 3 a.m. *I wouldn't dream of doing it any other way.*

Helper or Helpee?

My background is working with computers (Masters in Computer Information Systems), so I've always thought of myself as technologically competent. When the people at my Women's Group at my church asked for help with the audio/visual (AV) system, I volunteered. I thought I could be useful and it would be more interesting than just sitting there watching. This involved helping Janet with a laptop for PowerPoint words and music for our songs, microphones for the speakers, projector to display the PowerPoint words, DVD player, and sound board to control the sound for everything.

It seemed like it would be something I could handle, but it turned into another MSAdventure.

First of all, the command center for the A/V system in the back corner of the room was not exactly wheelchair accessible. The machines were tucked into the corner behind a tall cabinet/shelf homemade counter. The main shelf was about 4 feet high. To start with, all the miscellaneous stuff stored behind the counter had to be moved out before I could even get back there. The other people sat on tall stools to operate the equipment. Fortunately my fancy wheelchair had an option to elevate the seat about six inches. This allowed me to reach the shelf where the little laptop sat that controlled everything. No way could I fit into the corner to operate the soundboard.

All the switches to turn on the projector were in the front of the room behind the stage. Since I couldn't get past all the chairs, tables and stage to reach those switches, all I could do was watch as Janet did that part. She had written up very good instructions on how to set up everything. She patiently walked me through the procedure, describing what I couldn't reach or see.

Since all I could really get to was the laptop (barely), each week I would handle pressing the arrow keys to keep the words displayed on the projector in synch with the music while Janet did everything else. At least that was some help to her. This worked for the first couple of weeks. Then Janet informed me that she would be out the next week, so I would be running the WHOLE THING!

After my panic attack eased up a little I tried to pay attention to what she was saying. Everyone thought I would do just fine. Little did they know I was about to start my next MSAdventure.

As Murphy's Law for MS would tell it, all the switches to turn everything on and all the plugs and connectors were on a shelf too high or behind something I couldn't reach. So I had to enlist a helper. The obvious choice was Jean Ann, the friend who had just started driving me to church every Thursday morning. She was very willing to help, but old Murphy struck again – she was only five feet four inches tall, so she couldn't reach a lot of the connections either! So I had to ask another TALL girl who sat at our table to be my helper's helper.

On the day of my big debut as A/V person, we tried to get there early to get things set up, but of course got caught in traffic. When we got there, Jean Ann did great with all the switches up front. The connections on the A/V system were a bit more of a challenge. It was not easy to describe plugs and connectors that I had never seen to people that had never looked for them.

We managed to get things all set up and had the words showing up on the projector. I had even remembered the userid/password for the laptop. Only one minor problem – no sound! After we moved all the stools out of the tiny corner I was able to reach the sound board, but since I had never touched it before I obviously didn't know what I was doing. I tried, but no sound. This meant no music and no microphones for the leader or the speaker.

On top of that, the guest speaker had brought a DVD to be played as part of her presentation. Now I've operated a DVD before, and even though Janet had never shown me how to run a DVD, I thought I'd be able to handle it. However when I looked at the bottom shelf of "the rack" where I thought I had seen the DVD before, NO DVD player! This could be a problem.

A call went out to a guy on staff at the church who was supposed to be on call if we had any problems with the sound system. Could he be reached? Of course not! It was past time to get started, so the leader, who fortunately had a strong, beautiful voice, began the session without the microphone. The first song was a familiar one, so as I displayed the words, everyone sang a capella. The second song wasn't as well known, so we skipped that and went straight to the guest speaker.

While she began her presentation (talking loudly), the sound guy showed up. He found the DVD player – it had been pulled out of the rack and was sitting on a shelf where I couldn't even see it, much less reach it. He managed to find whatever switches I hadn't set correctly on the soundboard, and magically the speaker had a microphone that worked and we could watch her DVD – with picture and sound.

That's how I became the helpee instead of the helper. Next week when Janet is back, I'll try to figure out what I might have missed on the setup. I'll modify my little set of instructions, and *hope that Janet never misses a day again!*

Interruptions

A long time ago in Sunday school, I heard the story about Jonah being swallowed by a whale – and surviving! I didn't know there was a further lesson to this story.

The latest class in my Bible study group included a video series on Jonah. The interpretation of his life is that he was interrupted from his normal life to do something for God.

Has your life ever been interrupted like Jonah? This was the question asked by the leader of my class. I immediately knew my answer, but being my all-too-quiet, shy self, I didn't speak up. But I kept thinking about it.

My answer is a resounding "YES!" I thought I had my life generally planned out. Nothing spectacular, just a quiet, ordinary life. I had married the love of my life and with the addition of a beautiful little girl, we were building our family. I had envisioned raising our family, continuing to work at my computer job, going camping and enjoying an active lifestyle.

Then one afternoon as I was working at my computer, everything changed. I started having trouble seeing out of one of my eyes. By the end of the day I was blind in my right eye (see Chapter "How Did I Get Here?"). I didn't know it at the time, but my well-planned-out life was being interrupted. I was being swallowed by a huge, nasty whale called MS.

Just like Jonah, my life would never be the same again. Was this to be just a minor temporary interruption? This event occurred over 15 years ago, so "temporary" doesn't appear to fit this situation. Judging by the way my disability has increased, "minor" doesn't apply either.

So what's the purpose of this interruption to my otherwise ordinary life? That's what I keep trying to figure out. Do I have a message from God like Jonah did? If so, I'm still waiting to hear it so I can pass it on. I've met lots of people I wouldn't have met before and many of them are doctors or therapists who help me deal with all my problems. Weren't there already enough patients to go around?

Every now and then someone will tell me I inspire them. That one's really hard for me to see. Most days as I struggle along I feel anything but inspirational.

Since the purpose of this "interruption" continues to elude me, my only choice is to keep on going, trying to make the best of the situation. One day it will become clear, and I'll wonder why I didn't see it long ago - but probably not before I'm passing through the Pearly Gates.

My friends that have encouraged me to write this book tell me there are other people who would benefit from reading my story. If I could help just one person, then all the time and energy put into its creation would be worth it. On a side note, a cool $million for a New York Times best seller wouldn't be a bad thing either!

If the whole purpose of the journey was to write this book, I just have one question: *"Wasn't there another, perhaps easier, topic I could have written about?"*

Home Sweet Home

Most people go home to the same place every night. Sometimes it's necessary to get used to a different place to stay, at least temporarily.

This year 2012 didn't exactly start out according to plan. On December 30th, the paramedics rushed me to the hospital with a raging temperature of 93 degrees. Usually your body reacts to an infection by increasing your temperature to create a fever that will burn out the germs. Alternatively, it might just start shutting down, causing your temperature to drop significantly. Evidently this was what was happening to me.

In the hospital I was put on oxygen and IV antibiotics to treat pneumonia. My lungs were filled with fluid that had to be drained out with a very long needle, one lung at a time. Breathing treatments were needed every four hours. It was a long two weeks of treatments and many long scary nights waking up not knowing where I was, or how I got there or if I would be OK. Not the place I planned on celebrating New Year's Eve!

After two weeks my home changed to the rehab care center next to the hospital. There I continued breathing treatments and medicine. In addition I began three types of therapy every day. After breakfast each morning, I worked with Matt, the speech therapist. He attached four little electrodes to my throat which zapped my muscles to stimulate them as I performed swallowing exercises. Matt and his methods took me from thickened liquids and puréed food to normal food in four weeks, saving me from having to get a feeding tube.

While in rehab, I had daily occupational therapy (O.T.), dealing primarily with the arms and hands, and physical therapy (P.T.), working on the lower body. The nurses were caring and my roommates were mostly quite nice, but it still wasn't home, so there were many more long days and nights.

Rehab is where we celebrated our 30th wedding anniversary and Valentine's Day.

I fully planned on returning home next, but the insurance company decided to stop paying for rehab before my body was strong enough to be on my own at home. The pneumonia had taken its toll on my poor little body.

So we needed to find another place to continue my recuperation. The social worker at rehab recommended Charlene, whose job was to match up people with the appropriate housing accommodations. She worked with my husband, showing him three different homes in one night. They chose one of them, and I moved in the following day. This facility was a large home that had been extended to add more rooms. It was licensed for ten residents, but I would be number eight. My room was the master bedroom, large enough to hold my hospital bed, wheelchair and Hoyer lift (used to transfer me between the bed and the wheelchair).

This beautiful home had a lovely backyard where I entertained my visitors. The flowers were blooming even in February – after all, this is Arizona. The birds were singing in their little aviary. Some nights were still disturbing when I woke up, but after I realized where I was, I could usually get back to sleep. We paid for a month and agreed to thirty days notice for leaving, so I tried to settle in.

I thought the next stop would finally be home, but this was not to be. After only a week, a call came from our old friend, Charlene, saying that the owners requested that I find another place to live. I wondered what I could have done wrong. Even though my situation was difficult for me, I always tried to be pleasant and cooperative. It turns out that the Hoyer lift was too much for them to deal with. So my husband once again worked with Charlene to find me a new home. She was wonderful at easing the terrible stress of dealing with another very quick move.

The next day I was once again on the move. The new home was less than a mile away, so it didn't take very long. The people from the new place came with their truck and moved all my equipment (bed, lift, and wheelchair). I was soon settled into another group home with four other residents.

My room was smaller, but very homey and comfortable. The house always smelled wonderful from homemade soup cooking each day as well as other tasty dishes. Along with believing in natural foods, Susie, the main caregiver, used Aloe Vera instead of harsh medication to heal my skin problems.

This new place worked out to be a much better fit for me. The owners treated me like one of their family. If I couldn't be home, I was so glad I was there with such caring people. Sometimes things that are so terribly stressful turn out so much better than we anticipate.

I tried to relax and feel at home for a while. An Occupational Therapist and a Physical Therapist each came twice a week to continue my therapy. We worked on arm strengthening, sitting balance, and transferring using a slideboard. These were skills I would need before I could return home.

Soon it was St. Patrick's Day. I turned green with envy at other people who were in their own homes, and wished on a four-leaf-clover that I would soon do the same. *Maybe by Easter?*

Angels

The hardest thing for me to do is to talk in front of people, especially large groups. So last year when a friend asked me to speak at our church women's group, I immediately had a very un-Christian-like thought, something like, "Yeah, when you-know-where freezes over." But since she had just spent an hour helping me exercise my legs and was now massaging my swollen feet, I politely agreed to think about it. Then she hit me with the big one, "No pressure – God will let you know." Great, now I'm not only disappointing her, I'm disappointing God, too. No, no pressure. To my surprise, by the next day, I had a brief, typed outline, and a month later was in front of about 70 women. So all I can say is, the devil must have enjoyed his ice skates!

"Angels" – that's the idea that inspired me to speak. Angels don't need a robe, a harp, or even a halo. The first angel in my life was my Mom. She was the nicest, kindest person I've ever known. She always had a smile on her face and a kind word for everyone. About three years ago she got her harp and halo, and I know she's smiling down on us right now.

My husband, Steve, is one of my angels, although some days I might have other names for him. MS is a challenge for both of us. He has stuck by me through it and built ramps or whatever else I needed. From the time my daughter, Laura, was born, I knew she was an angel on loan from God, bringing so much joy into my life. As soon as she got her driver's license, my leg was affected by MS, so she began driving me around, and continues to do whatever she can to support me.

If it's printed on a notepad, it must be true, right? This is what my notepad says, "Friends are angels following you through life." I've been blessed with such wonderful friends. Some angels play guitars instead of harps, like my friend LuAnn. "My MSAdventures" began as emails to her describing my day. Her slightly warped sense of humor helped me through some tough times by showing me how to laugh and make fun of things instead of just whining. These emails became the start of this book.

When I began having physical therapy at home, the therapist asked if I had any friends who would help me on days when she didn't come. The therapist trained Lorette, who then organized a small group to help me. I automatically called this group my "therapy angels." I figured that anyone who was willing to spend their time and their gasoline to come over and rub my ugly feet had to be an angel!

Some angels use airplane wings instead of their own. My high school friend, Jan, who now lives in California, flies over for a long weekend each year just to visit with me in Phoenix - in AUGUST! You can't tell me that's not an angel!

Other angels use the airwaves to send electronic greetings and emails to keep in touch and brighten my day. They have sent postcards or letters or even called while on vacation. Just to know someone cares and is thinking about you does so much to relieve anxiety and depression.

Angels can even be disguised as bus drivers. One of my favorite drivers is a great big guy named Alvin. He has a stuffed Chipmunks doll on the dashboard. He has a big smile and makes me feel special. I always get him when I'm having an especially tough morning. That can't just be a coincidence.

It amazes me how many times the drivers have Christian music playing, and how caring they are to me. One day I had a new driver, who talked the whole way about God. When we got to my house, she asked if she could say a prayer for me. She knelt down next to my scooter in the bus and prayed hard for 5 minutes, tears streaming down her face. I wish I knew what she had said – most of it was in Spanish, which I don't speak – but I knew she was praying for a miracle for me. I didn't start the conversation or tell her anything about myself, so I either looked really pathetic, or she was another angel sent to me.

One of the only things that really ease my stiff, aching body is a massage. When I went to get a massage, I was randomly assigned a terrific lady named Sharon. She has 4 boys, and just does massage part-time because she thinks it helps people. She's become a good friend – we talk the whole time. Turns out she belongs to my church. She's even coming in on her day off just to give me a massage because I told her how stiff physical therapy made me. A coincidence that I was assigned to her – or another angel sent to me?

I'd seen Lorette at women's functions for a few years, but didn't really get to know her well until recently. This last year has been very difficult for me, but she's done so much to help me get through it. She came to visit me a lot in the rehab hospital, sent postcards from Australia & New Zealand, and called me from Florida on her vacation. When I started having physical therapy at home, she organized my "therapy angels."

The ironic thing I realized is over the past couple of years, when Lorette has given me little gifts, such as pins or knickknacks, they've all been angels – but really, she's been my angel, herself.

When I was asked to speak at our women's group, I didn't know how I could think of two minutes worth, much less 20. But as I started thinking of all the angels in my life, the list got longer & longer. I was astounded by all the angels that kept coming to mind.

You never know when you are going to meet an angel. Angels are everywhere. Open your mind and you will be amazed and encouraged.

So if you've ever wondered if angels really exist, I can assure you they do. In fact I can tell you how to find them. *Just look into any mirror and you'll see one!*

Black Hole

Through all the MSAdventures I've lived through, I've come to one conclusion: MS is not for sissies!

To fight this battle you must be strong, brave, and definitely maintain a sense of humor. The question is, "So how do you stay upbeat and happy all the time in spite of your problems?" Answer: "You don't." – at least not all the time.

There will be times, unfortunately many times, when you want to lash out in anger at the world or cry your heart out or just give up. Sometimes I can feel myself spiraling downwards into what I call my "black hole."

What starts me heading into the abyss? It could be anything: a major exacerbation (fancy MS techno-talk for symptoms worsening), an invitation to some function I won't be able to attend, or just a look from a stranger at my wheelchair.

When I first started limping, I needed to face buying a cane. Sounds like a simple task, but it tore me up inside.

Forty-two years old, and I was buying a cane for goodness sake! I learned then to do whatever I could to ease the transition to any necessary "adjustment" to my life.

MS is a progressive disease. The next step in my progression was from the cane to a walker. A walker!!! They're for old, crippled people, not a young Mom like me!

The transition to a little 3-wheeled scooter was much easier. Scooters were cute and powerful, and let me move quickly and as far as the battery would take me. This opened up more activities again because I could keep up with and sometimes outlast my two-legged friends.

As I moved on to the scooter, my daughter had her own life-changing transition – she became a licensed driver! Being the wonderful, supportive Mom that I am, I let her drive whenever we were out together. At about the same time my right leg became weaker. My daughter soon began driving me around all the time.

Giving up driving still hurts ten years later. Next week I will officially change my driver's license into an ID card. So many things would be so simple if I could still drive. Every time I need to see a doctor or go anywhere or do anything, I have to coordinate it with someone else's schedule. I have a complicated spreadsheet on my computer to track all my appointments and associated drivers. Not only do they need to drive, but they must drive my van in order to take my wheelchair. We bought a new van several years ago equipped with a ramp. It's frustrating to know I'll never drive it.

So many things I used to enjoy doing. I taught swimming, canoeing and sailing. We used to race our little sailboat. I would control the boat while Steve balanced on a trapeze to keep the boat from tipping over. I loved the sound (or lack thereof) when we shut off the little motor and unfurled the sails.

The three of us enjoyed camping with our little pop-up camper. We would meet my sister on a mountain in Colorado each summer or just find a place in the forest or desert in Arizona. But the camper wasn't exactly wheelchair compatible.

Singing along with my guitar by the campfire was a real joy. Now my hands can't hold the guitar, and MS has affected my voice.

From the time I was in college and spent a semester abroad in Scotland, traveling has been a source of pleasure. However between accommodations for my wheelchair and other problems, travel, especially flying, is very difficult now.

MS has stolen many things away from me. Precious things. Happy things.

But the one thing it can't steal is who I am on the inside. My friend, Lorette, keeps telling me, "You're still Becky, being in a wheelchair doesn't change that." Sometimes that's hard to remember, because I don't feel like myself any more.

So what's left? Even though we don't go camping together any more, and my daughter has grown up, gone to college, and moved away to find a job, we are still a close family. Instead of sailing away, my husband and I enjoy watching science fiction movies on TV and going to a baseball game.

I'm so blessed to have wonderful friends. They don't care if I'm in a wheelchair or have MS. Some I've even met because I have MS.

Even though I can't type 60 words per minute like I used to (now it's one finger at a time), I've written a book! People are actually asking me to come and speak at their meetings – and willing to pay me to do so!

One of the best ways to stop feeling bad about what I've lost is to think of ways I could help others. It amazes me that I still can do that. From my wheelchair or even in bed, I can send an email, make a phone call, say a prayer, or just listen to someone else talk about their day or their problems. These sound like little insignificant things, but they can make a big difference in someone else's life, as well as adding meaning and joy to my own.

I can still be a wife, a mother, and a friend.

They say if one door closes, and another doesn't open, try a window!

It takes courage and sometimes creativity to find new ways to live your life when things change beyond your control, but it's so worth it!

So climb out of your black hole. When you feel yourself spiraling downward into the abyss, just don't go there. Call a friend. Turn on the TV. Think of something you can do for someone else.

Every morning make this the best day you can. Don't waste a minute of it!

So I can't drive any more – let it go, and enjoy the people who are happy to do the driving.

So we don't go camping or sailing any more – let it go. We still have each other and can find new things to enjoy together.

So I can't type with two hands any more – let it go. I've written a book!

Whatever you've lost, mourn it if you need to, then LET IT GO! *More adventures or MSAdventures are still ahead.*

More MSAdventures Ahead

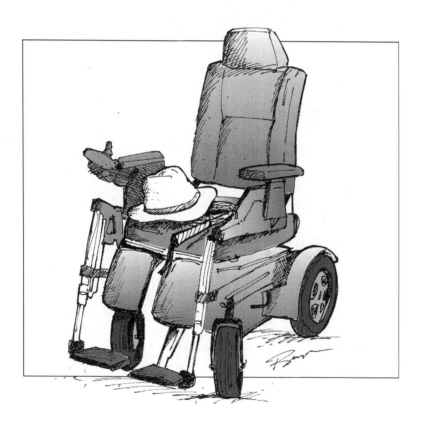

So Where Do I Go From Here?

One guarantee comes with having MS: you will have an endless supply of adventures awaiting you. So how will you handle them – with humor? With frustration? With depression? All of the above?

Unfortunately you can't change your circumstances. What you **do** have control over is your attitude (see chapter "Changes in Latitude"), and the way you deal with the situation. So you're not the same person you were before you got MS – who will you be?

Are you going to turn into that whiny, depressing person that no one wants to be around? Or will you make the best of an awful situation by getting involved and becoming an inspiration to others? Something in-between?

My brother, Dave, has MS, too. He's also had other problems throughout his life, as we all do, but in spite of everything he's been through, he always seems to be in a good mood. I asked him how he stays that way. He told me that he's going to have problems. He can either be cheerful or miserable - he will still have the same problems. He would rather be cheerful.

Being depressed and miserable is the easy way, but not a fun life. Instead search for fun things to do with your life and people to do them with. Look for laughter. I found an organization that developed something called "laughter yoga." I bought the DVD from the website. It's fun to do either by yourself or with friends.

Use your imagination to find ways to connect with others, either special people like yourself or "regular people" with their own problems. Everyone needs friends to share problems, do activities with or just to talk to or laugh with.

So you're not the same person you used to be – no one is! Who will you be? *Go out there and enjoy having some MSAdventures!*

Appendix

Useful MS websites

National MS Society
    www.nmss.org
    (contains links to other chapters)

Arizona MS Society
    aza.nationalmssociety.org

Rocky Mountain Chapter
    www.mscenter.org

Multiple Sclerosis Information
    www.MSlifelines.com
    www.MSActiveSource.com

Store for special shoes and other products
    www.hamiltonprosthetics.com

Made in the USA
Lexington, KY
21 September 2015